HOMEBUILDING & RENOVATING

BOOK OF

GREAT VALUE
SELF-BUILD HOMES

24 INSPIRING HOMES BUILT FROM £32,000–£150,000

Ascent Publishing Limited
A CENTAUR COMMUNICATIONS COMPANY

Sugar Brook Court, Aston Road,
Bromsgrove, Worcestershire, B60 3EX
Tel: 01527 834400 Fax: 01527 834497
E-mail: homebuilding@centaur.co.uk

COVER PHOTOGRAPHY: ROB JUDGES

BACK COVER PHOTOGRAPHY: NIGEL RIGDEN & JEREMY PHILLIPS

PUBLISHED BY ASCENT PUBLISHING LIMITED

2 SUGAR BROOK COURT

ASTON ROAD, BROMSGROVE

WORCESTERSHIRE

B60 3EX

© 2003 ASCENT PUBLISHING LIMITED

ALL RIGHTS RESERVED

FIRST PRINTING (SOFT COVER) 2003

ISBN 0-9544669-0-X

PRINTED IN CHINA BY PHOENIX OFFSET

REPRINTED 2004

PRODUCED BY

www.homebuilding.co.uk

homebuilding@centaur.co.uk

CONTENTS

CONTENTS

FOREWORD

Since 1990 when *Homebuilding & Renovating* magazine was born (it was known as *Individual Homes* in those days) the amount of interest in the idea of individuals creating a unique home for themselves has enjoyed phenomenal growth. These people are often referred to as 'self-builders' although this is partially a misleading term. It conjures up visions of pioneering folk in wellington boots living in a caravan on a muddy and cold building site doing all the construction work themselves on their DIY home.

Such brave souls exist but self-build does not have to be like this. Most people who build their own home will either appoint an architect or designer to design their home and a builder to construct it or they will hire in sub-contractors (bricklayers, roofers, carpenters, plumbers, electricians etc.) to carry out the individual tasks under their own project management. Many people will do some DIY themselves – perhaps the decorating – but some will do nothing physical at all, preferring to believe that DIY is translated as 'Don't Involve Yourself'!

A whole industry of suppliers from specialist mortgage lenders and plot finding agencies to package build companies offering to guide you through the whole process, has sprung up to meet the needs of people wanting to build for themselves.

As publisher of Homebuilding & Renovating magazine, I have seen hundreds of new self-build homes from all parts of the UK, built by people from all walks of life. One thing they have in common is that they want to maximise their quality of life in a home that minimises their financial commitment to the project. This can mean wiping out a hefty mortgage or getting the most for your money from limited resources; it can mean gaining a first step on the housing ladder, or perhaps building a low cost home for retirement.

Unlike buying from a developer, you don't have to sacrifice space when self-building; you don't have to take a long time to build a new home; you don't have to choose a modest location and you certainly don't have to build a standard 'box' house. All of these 24 projects prove, in different ways, that a modest budget does not have to mean a modest house.

Peter Harris
Publishing Director
Ascent Publishing Limited

The homes featured in this book appeared originally in Homebuilding & Renovating Magazine. The build costs range from an astonishing £32,000 to £150,000. Each of the projects featured includes floor plans, cost details and contacts as well as detailed interviews with the self builders. If you are interested in having a quality home designed and built to your own specifications and, importantly, budget, then this book is definitely for you. There is also a series of 18 features about doing DIY on your self-Build project.

Economy Class

Sue Hobbs' new home in Salcombe, Devon, combines a beautiful oak framed first floor with a traditional blockwork ground floor below.

Words:
Clive Fewins

Photography:
Nigel Rigden

The wooden ▶ floor has been painted with a thinned down white emulsion to give it a lighter look.

Sue Hobbs' small two storey house in a shady corner of a steep lane leading out of the Devon town of Salcombe is proof that you can incorporate an oak frame into your self-build without spending much more than you would with conventional brick and block construction. The final price when Sue moved in during the summer of 1999 was £686/m² – a very reasonable figure when you bear in mind that Salcombe is a highly desirable town where property prices are high and the house, which cost £103,000 to build, is already worth an estimated £325,000.

It is even more of a financial achievement when you consider that Sue, a retired administrator, paid the modest asking price of £40,000 for the plot as soon as she saw it. "I just knew it was too good an opportunity to miss, especially in an area where undeveloped plots like this are extremely rare," she says.

▶

An oak frame home built on a modest budget

"[The build price] is a remarkable figure for a house that everybody seems to think is very imaginative..."

The internal ▶ bridge balcony forms the spine of the house from the main living room to the master bedroom.

The one sixth of an acre plot is away from the centre of the town and lacks views of the estuary. It does however face south and has a fine view through woods over the tower of the parish church to the other side of the estuary. Rather than taking its inspiration from the water, it derives much of its character from the trees that surround it, which is one reason why the oak framed upper storey seemed so appropriate.

Sue, a widow, could not afford an entire house built with an oak frame so architect and oak frame specialist Roderick James created a cavity-walled masonry structure to first floor ceiling height.

There was however a planning problem at the outset. A near neighbour objected on the grounds that the existing planning permission that came with the site was for a bungalow and not a two-storey dwelling. By the use of a graph showing the precise sites of existing houses on the steeply-sloping hillside, Sue and Roderick were able to show that the house would not block the view of the neighbour in question.

The foundations proved difficult. Because of the soft nature of the ground on the sloping site it was necessary to use 15ft deep mass concrete footings. "This cost me £10,000 — about £5,000 more than I expected," says Sue.

Sewage disposal also caused difficulties. Because of the terrain and the proximity to a graveyard, a septic tank was not permitted and the sewage has to be pumped to the sewer 100 metres up the road. This meant a 90 metre excavation along the footpath. The cost? An extra £5,000.

"Despite all this the final build figure still came to only £103,000," says Sue. "Even at 1999 prices I still feel it was a remarkable figure for a house that everybody seems to think is beautifully designed and laid out, and a very imaginative and contemporary rendering of a traditional means of construction."

The house is certainly that. It is feels minimalist, although Sue prefers the word "internationalist." There are no architraves and no skirting. The internal walls have a rough plastered finish and are painted white.

To save expense the glazing is set into the frame by a system of toughened double glazing and oak cover boards. The main heating is underfloor and by means of the log burning stove in the main living room. There are radiators only in the two bathrooms.

All the emphasis on the first floor is on the timber frame, with the main bedroom, reception room and kitchen upstairs all constructed in this way. The cathedral ceiling soars above the small interior, the boards painted an attractive terracotta colour on the inside. Above this is a thick layer of insulation and a roof of reclaimed Welsh slate, punctuated by two sets of rooflights front and rear that allow light to flood in.

Roderick has also managed to bring light into the solid masonry ground floor by using a whole array of deep narrow bespoke rooflights that sweep over a clever linking internal bridge balcony. This runs from the main reception room and living area through to the master bedroom via the kitchen and crosses over the hallway beneath. It is reminiscent of a ship's gangplank and the wooden floor, painted with white emulsion thinned down with water, adds to the nautical feel.

▶

Useful Contacts

Architect – Roderick James: 01803 722474

Builder – Roy Chapman: 01548 521266

Frame – Carpenter Oak Ltd: 01803 732900

Landscaping – MGM Nurseries: 01548 550754

Fact File costs as of April 2002

NAME: Sue Hobbs

PROFESSION: Retired

AREA: South Devon

HOUSE TYPE: Three bedrooms on two floors

HOUSE SIZE: 150m²

BUILD ROUTE: Main contractor

CONSTRUCTION: Oak frame with masonry ground floor

WARRANTY: None

SAP RATING: 84

FINANCE: Private

BUILD TIME: Six months
LAND COST: £40,000

BUILD COST: £103,000

TOTAL COST: £143,000

CURRENT VALUE: £325,000

COST/m²: £686

56% COST SAVING

Cost Breakdown:

Main building contract	£60,000
Oak Frame	£25,000
Groundworks etc	£10,000
Sewage Works	£5,000
Miscellaneous	£3,000
TOTAL	**£143,000**

The staircase has concrete treads surmounted with clay tiles that give it a Mediterranean feel. This descends to the two spare bedrooms and bathroom in the masonry built ground floor, which is covered with the same tiles.

Outside there is a similarly uncluttered feel. The rustic steps are created from half telegraph poles with gravel behind and ascend to a patio area that is accessed from an opening glazed window positioned by the side of the fireplace. It continues round the end of the house to merge into the decking that forms the front balcony.

"The effect inside in the daytime is brilliant… the light swirls around…"

The glazed door which leads from the balcony to the main reception room is frequently used as the front door and has in some ways supplanted the true front door next to the garage on the ground level. The latter is a practical affair, but is easily overlooked compared with the first floor means of entry, which many find much more appealing. To counter this, Sue is planning to install a downstairs porch in order to point the way to the true front door. The steps, balcony and means of entry are all designed to make the most of the southerly aspect of the building.

The view from the front is of a steeply-pitched roof with prominent oak bargeboards and an external chimney with glazed panels on either side. Where there are no windows there is treated softwood weatherboarding. The external balustrading that surrounds the deck above the garage blends well with all the glass and creates a striking effect at the front.

"I wanted lots of wood interspersed with glass and it works extremely well," says Sue. "The effect inside during the daytime is brilliant. On a bright day the light swirls around and creates dappled patterns on the walls. Even on a dull day you can see the clouds go scudding by through all the glass and at night there is a completely different feel as the spotlights shine upwards towards all that lovely oak.

"It is a house that is designed to fit the sloping site and the nature of the landscape, as well as being just the right size for one person. There are also all sorts of clever features such as the glazed walls on either side of the inglenook and the storage loft above the kitchen which is accessed by a ladder. It is also possible to accommodate my four grandchildren when they come to stay.

"It is very warm in winter but possible to create a beautiful breeze by opening all the doors in summer. For many years I knew all about Roderick's work and yearned for a house like this. But I really never thought I would be able to afford one." ■

First Floor

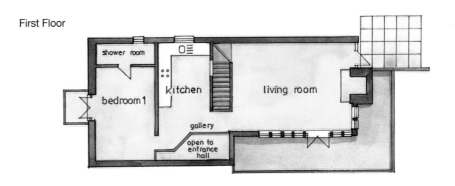

Ground Floor

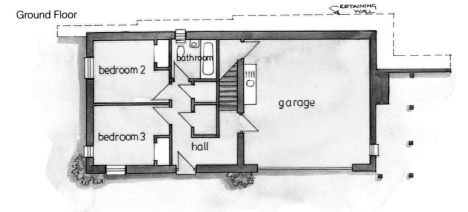

A SENSE

A modern open plan bungalow

In what was formerly her garden, Audrey Ogg
has built a new home for her retirement —
a modern and spacious single storey property
designed by her architect son Graham.

Words: **Jude Webley**   Pictures: **Douglas Gibb**

OF SPACE

This strikingly contemporary house nestling in the Perthshire hills was designed and built for Audrey Ogg as a retirement home by her son, Graham. Offering a marked contrast to the huge Victorian villas which are its neighbours, Graham was determined to inject progressive thinking into the design of the house yet link it to historical tradition.

"The house is much more closely derived from the traditional, white walled, single storey crofter's cottage but in a modern form," he explains. "When I was preparing the planning application I had to put forward the case that the design was similar in proportion and scale to the old cottages. By showing the planners old photographs and drawings I was able to convince them that the design had historical precedents in the area."

It turns out that a guideline issued by The Scottish Executive (PPG Housing in the Countryside) is in favour of encouraging contemporary design, although by no means all the Planning Officers are aware of this or sympathetic to it.

Originally Audrey and her husband, who died in 1980, had moved to the area to run a guest house next door to the new property. There was outline planning for two

▲ The south facing rear of the property houses the open plan living area. Two large glazed doors link inside and out.

▶

▲ Generously proportioned glazed doors in the southern elevation ensure the living area is light and airy.

The open plan living area is loosely defined into two zones, a cooking and eating area to one side and sitting room to the other.

houses in the grounds which Audrey, wisely, kept renewing. When running the guest house became too much for her, she decided to build herself. If you're thinking of building a house, having an architect for a son is a pretty good start. If you're an up and coming architect, hungry for interesting and challenging commissions, having the opportunity of designing a house for your mother is a pretty good career move.

Together Audrey and Graham have created a superb contemporary home in which Audrey is delighted to spend her retirement. "I had certain ideas of what I wanted but in reality I gave Graham pretty much a free hand," she explains. "Even if I might once have disagreed with some of his ideas, having lived in the house for a couple of years I find that it suits me very well."

"'After all, if you're building a one off home where nothing is standard, why bother with a kit manufacturer?"

The design and structure are unusual. Twin pitched roofs with a low ridge height are joined by an area of flat roof. The internal layout of the house is based on a central 'route' running from the front door (and garage door) at the north end to the largely glazed elevation of the open plan living space incorporating kitchen, dining area and lounge area at the south. Here, the large glazed sliding doors help blur the boundaries between house and garden – especially in summer.

"The route is more than just a means of circulation, more than a corridor," explains Audrey. "It is a wider space in which I can house some furniture which has great sentimental value for me. It creates a sense of openness throughout the house and provides an area for my grandchildren to play in. At night I particularly like the way the moonlight enters the centre of the house through the rooflights."

Graham worked closely with his structural engineer, David Scott, to determine the best way of constructing the design. "David has a design approach to engineering," explains Graham. He came up with and costed a number of solutions before the decision was made to go for a post and beam, timber frame approach with regular spans based on practical details, like the size of standard sheets of plasterboard in order to eliminate waste from the construction process.

Internally, some unusual techniques were used. The cladding of the stud walls of the central 'route' used squares of plywood screwed on to noggins, with gaps left exposed creating an oriental feeling. The plasterboard ceiling panes were treated in a similar way. A 'shadowgap' detail technique was used to replace the need for conventional skirtings and architrave around internal doors — 820mm (wider than normal) plain fire doors, used because they are attractively heavy.

The planning process took an impressively short eight weeks and Graham put the project out to competitive tender from main contractors based on a fully specified brief. On site, however, things did not always go smoothly.

"Because we are working in a part of Scotland where timber frame is the accepted way of doing things and there are plenty of skilled joiners who understand the techniques, I always like to use a local joiner to stick build on site rather than a timber frame kit manufacturer," he explains. "After all, if you're building a one off home where nothing is standard, why bother with a kit manufacturer?"

As is so often the case in building projects, the problems were largely ones of communication. According to Graham, the appointed main contractor could have thought through the design more thoroughly before starting work. In any event, the main contractor subcontracted a great ▶

The main route through the house is not a corridor, Audrey insists, but an area that stands alone as a living space.

▲ The sense of spaciousness in the open plan living area is enhanced by the lofty vaulted ceilings.

The route continues into the spacious open plan living area, defined by the lower ceiling height and structural posts

deal of the work to a joiner, adding further complexity to the chain of command.

"In larger commercial projects," says Graham, "there are necessary systems of contract administration that are costed into the job. Suffice it to say that on a smaller job the lines of communication can become very cumbersome when you have to deal with a main contractor and then his appointed subcontractor. On my next housing commission — another small new house — I worked with a client who wanted to employ subcontractors himself in defined and costed packages of work. On balance I'd say that this approach was more efficient."

This was an excellent opportunity for a young architect to show what he can do. Not only has Graham succeeded in delivering for his mother a really pleasant low maintenance environment in which to spend her later years, but he's pushed the boundaries of contemporary house design in a practical and visually exciting way.

His next project, which is now more or less complete, is another high quality, civilised small house. In a quiet, unpretentious and extremely thoughtful way, Graham Ogg is showing himself capable of delivering what a growing minority of people might want in a house but find hard to achieve — practical, contemporary style that blends harmoniously in its environment and is far more than mere metropolitan ostentation. ■

The internal layout of the house is based on a central 'route' ▶ running from the front door at the north end to the almost entirely glazed elevation of the open plan living space incorporating kitchen, dining area and lounge area at the south.

Fact File costs as of March 2001

NAME: Audrey Ogg

PROFESSION: Retired

AREA: Perthshire

HOUSE TYPE: Single storey

HOUSE SIZE: 115m²

BUILD ROUTE: Architect and contractor

CONSTRUCTION: Stick built timber frame

FINANCE: Private

BUILD TIME: Seven months

LAND COST: £30,000 (already owned)

BUILD COST: £91,000

TOTAL COST: £121,000

COST/M²: £790

HOUSE VALUE: £170,000

29% COST SAVING

Useful Contacts

Architect — Graham Ogg: 01796 472240

Main Contractor — Burnside Joiners and Contractors: 01887 829556

Roof Slates — Redland Roofing Systems: 08705 601000

Pyramidical Rooflights — Coxdome Ltd: 01442 824222

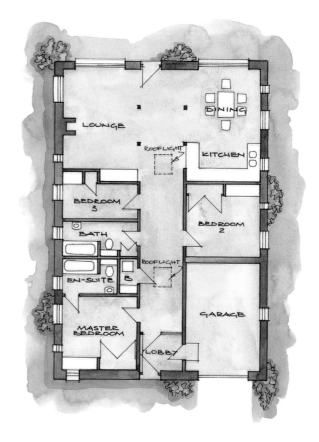

▼ The front elevation of the home displays its roots in the traditional Scottish crofter's cottage — transformed for the 21st Century.

DIY Bricklaying

Being let down by a series of subcontractors forced Don Ramsden to do the bulk of the work on his first self-build himself — at the age of 71.

You'd think that at the age of 71 most people would want to put their feet up but not Don Ramsden and his wife Freda. They not only embarked on a self-build project but Don elected to do quite a bit of the work himself.

They'd wanted to build their own home for quite a while and as Don says, "it was just unfortunate that I happened to be 71 by the time we were able to do so." They were gazumped on the first plot they found but then discovered a multiple site for £60,000 which they split into three, selling one plot off and the other to their son. Their total build costs for the 185m², three bedroom property plus double garage and conservatory came to £80,000 and it is now valued at somewhere in the region of £130,000.

The house was built using a timber frame from Guardian Homes Ltd. Don has done the beam and block ground floor and infill, the ducting for the central heating, all the plumbing and central heating, the tacking and insulation, the wooden flooring throughout the house, the brickwork to the inglenook, and the whole of the garage.

You built your own home using subcontractors so why did you elect to build the garage by yourself?

I hadn't planned to. I'd always hoped to do the other bits and pieces in the house but it was really when the house was finished that I was thrust into it. The builders had left the garage as just a slab and they kept saying they would come back but they didn't, so I thought, why not get on and do it myself?

I'd done the inglenook fireplace and found that I quite liked laying bricks. It's not rocket science. I couldn't use a line on the fireplace but I got things just about right and dead level for the Bessemer beam — and that was only using a level. There's quite a bit of detail in that and I got better as I went along. After that I decided that I'd do the dwarf walls for the conservatory.

That was entirely different but I was able to practice laying to a line and when the guys didn't turn up to do the garage, I thought I'd do it myself.

It's one thing doing a fireplace and a few walls but quite another building a double garage — that's almost like a small bungalow.

You're right, if you look you'll see that it's a cavity wall construction as well. Still, the principle is the same. The thing to do is get the corners level and to keep using your gauge. I made that myself by measuring off the brickwork on the house and it served me well.

for £100 per day but on the Friday he cried off. I thought, here we go again. I asked my son to help me get them up onto the plate and it took

"I'd wanted to build my own home for some time... it was just that I happened to be 71 before I was able to!"

Once you've got the corners up you can put a line from one to the other and just fill in. From then on it's plain sailing. It had to be right, or I'd take it down and do it again.

Lifting the steel lintels up was a bit of a struggle by myself, but I did it. It was the same with the stone features that sit into the lintels. A representative from a truss company was driving by and he stopped and asked me if I'd ordered the trusses. I told him I'd built the garage myself and he couldn't believe it, especially when he measured up and found that it was square.

You'd only intended to do the brickwork and leave the roof to others?

That was the plan but once again I was let down. I bought the trusses from the chap who dropped in and as they were big and heavy I got quotes from two joiners. One said that he'd come the next day at 10am. I never saw him again. Another said he'd do it at the weekend

the two of us four hours to brace and nail them ready for the gable ends.

I didn't cut the bricks up the gables as we've got boxed verges but I did have to make my own gable ladders at each end. In the end most things like this come down to common sense and following the plans. I didn't tile the roof. The tiler who had done the house had priced for the garage as well and he didn't let us down.

Did you hang the garage doors yourself as well?

I hung every other door in the house so why not them? Shooting doors isn't a problem, but Freda helped me with the main garage doors. They are cantilevered 'up and over' doors and if you just follow the instructions it's easy. They just screw to the frames and as long as they're upright and fixed in the right plane you're all right. The springs are pre-tensioned and you take a pin out to release them. ∎

A FARMYARD TALE
Building a Georgian style farmhouse from scratch

Self-builders Paul Sargeantson and Fiona Elliott have created a beautiful Georgian style farmhouse near Oxford that nobody believes is brand new.

It could almost be a scene from *The Darling Buds of May*. A large farmyard, chickens coming and going from a huge old wooden henhouse, horses, dogs, a pond, an aura of gentle decay – and an early Georgian farmhouse. It is now a complete picture again thanks to self-builders Paul Sargeantson and Fiona Elliott, who have brought the farmyard back to life after years of neglect.

It might be hard to believe that Paul and Fiona are self-builders rather than renovators – but while the barns, cattle shed and granary date back to the 18th century, the house is a meticulous recreation of an early Georgian brick farmhouse. Built in the style of the area – South Oxfordshire – it blends in seamlessly with the timber-framed and tiled surrounding agricultural buildings to complete the farmyard group.

When they had the opportunity to buy the yard and dilapidated buildings in 1993 Paul and Fiona, who were highly commended in the Best Traditional House section of The Daily Telegraph/Homebuilding & Renovating Awards 2001, jumped at it. They paid £65,000 for the yard and 28 acres of land, part of an estate at the foot of the Oxfordshire Chilterns that was being broken up and sold.

They paid for it with the proceeds of their house in the nearby village of Watlington, which they managed to sell quickly before moving into a rented house nearby. They then set about getting planning permission – not an easy task as they had been told that planning permission would be contrary to the Local Plan.

"Our local planning authority has a reputation for being 'sticky' when it comes to gaining planning permission,"

Words:
Clive Fewins

Photography:
Rob Judges

▶

▲ French doors in the living room lead to a deck at the rear of the property. The timber fire surround was made by a local joiner.

says Fiona, a farm secretary. "I work with land agents and several of them indicated that we were daft to take such a risk and would not get consent."

Although the planning officer they dealt with was behind the proposal and recommended it for approval, Paul and Fiona decided to take no risks and set about lobbying members of the planning committee in an attempt to commend the scheme to them.

"You could say that we are in favour of managed neglect…. We do not like things over-gentrified…."

"We were desperately anxious not to go for a barn conversion," says Paul. "Several knowledgeable friends had said they thought this was all we would get. We are country lovers and traditionalists and like to keep our barns as barns. You could say that we are in favour of managed neglect in the countryside. We do not like things so over-gentrified that they become suburban-looking."

Fortunately by visiting several members of the planning committee and inviting others to see the site they managed to convince the councillors that the house they had in mind would enhance and complement the group of farmyard buildings – and duly gained planning consent. "Basically we have inserted an early 18th century brick farmhouse into a traditional farmyard. We think it is in perfect harmony with the surroundings," says Paul. ▶

The kitchen and utility room occupy a single storey annexe at the side of the house. The Alpha range also provides hot water.

"I just can't help collecting these lovely old materials and items when I come across them..."

▲ The quality of the brickwork is extremely high. The reclaimed bricks are laid in Flemish bond with lime mortar. The arches and dentil course are in keeping with houses of the 17th century.

The scheme was the idea of Paul and Fiona, plus Paul's Herefordshire-based brother Andrew, who carried out the design with the aid of architectural technician John Henderson, sadly now deceased. Local conservation officer Peter Mills advised on detailing. "The idea was to make it look absolutely what one would expect in that setting and we have achieved it," says Paul. "The trade-off for the local council was that the estate was being split up and the barns needed a raison d'etre. They were not keen on the barns being converted to residential use and part of the deal was that we would restore them."

It was a long project. The actual build took 18 months and was held up in the middle by mortgage problems. Lloyds TSB withdrew their self-build product in England and Wales (they still operate in Scotland) for reasons that Paul and Fiona still can't quite understand, just at the time they had found exactly the bricks they wanted in the right

quantity at a local reclamation yard. Funds were so tight that they had to borrow some family money to secure the bricks until the new loan they had negotiated with the Norwich and Peterborough Building Society came through.

Paul put in all the foundations and the septic tank as well as installing the floor joists and roof trusses, laying the floorboards and fixing the plasterboard. He also carried out the repairs to agricultural buildings, moving his fencing business to the largest of the barns. Another barn now serves as stabling for their two horses and in the others Paul stores his large collection of second hand furniture and architectural pieces. All the internal doors came from his stock.

"I just can't help collecting these lovely old materials and items when I come across them," he says. "We have managed to incorporate some of them in the house – for example the outside lights and the square terracotta floor tiles in the downstairs cloakroom."

The layout of the house revolves round the elegant pitch pine staircase made for them, together with the drawing room fire surround and all the windows, by local joiner Andrew Hicks, who has now retired.

The kitchen and utility room are on one level with vaulted ceilings that open up to the roof. This section of the building is slightly stepped back from the two-storey section of the house because it joins onto a long woodshed with an open frontage supported by oak pillars, while on the other side of the yard is the cartshed that houses the stables.

But it is the outside of the house that Paul and Fiona find the most pleasing. This is because the Flemish bond brickwork – created by master bricklayer John Sweetzer using alternative headers and stretchers in the same course – perfectly resembles the style of the early Georgian farmhouses in that part of Oxfordshire. John paid great attention not only to the bond, but also to the jointing, ▶

Useful Contacts

Structural engineer — JJ Associates:		01491 614148
Technical consultancy — Andrew Sargeantson:		07774 158196
Master bricklayer — John Sweetzer:		01189 411030
Electrics — Oxford Electrical:		01865 376362
Plumber — Leighton Greenslade:		01865 890691
Reclaimed bricks and tiles — D J Giles:		01494 482396:
Boiler/cooker — Alpha:		01635 582068
Second fix carpentry — Peter Dove:		01189 722225
Plasterer — Dick Quelch:		01491 641542
Ironwork — Turnpike Forge:		01865 407755

The hall floor is laid in natural
limestone. The beautiful
encaustic tiles in the
downstairs cloakroom were
found in a reclamation yard.

First Floor

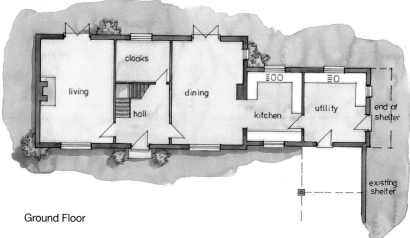

Ground Floor

leaving the mortar to go off and using a stiff brush a day or two later to expose the aggregate. The bricklayers even started out slaking their own lime for the mortar but when they found this too laborious they switched to bagged lime.

Another traditional feature is the reclaimed cast iron guttering, which Paul managed to obtain for just over £200 from the reclamation yard where he obtained the bricks. The fine brackets with thin stays that support the guttering cost twice as much and were made at a local forge. The roof is of reclaimed handmade clay peg tiles — again sourced locally.

"There is the potential for two more bedrooms if they need them as they have constructed the roof using attic trusses."

They have finished up with a house of 198m[2] on two floors with conventional oil-fired central heating and three bedrooms, the master being en suite. However, there is potential for two more bedrooms if ever they need them as they have constructed the roof using attic trusses with sections of cut roof in between that can accommodate possible future dormer windows. The staircase has also been designed so that it could be extended to a third floor.

"We are delighted the way the whole project has come together," says Paul. "And of course it gives us enormous satisfaction when people who pass by just don't realise it is a completely new house. There are times when we look at this place and still can't believe the huge dollop of good luck we had in finding it with all its surrounding acres." ∎

FLOORPLAN: The main section of the house is arranged as a traditional Georgian farmhouse would have been, with a central hallway, living room to one side and dining room to the other. The kitchen and utility room occupy a single storey annexe and feature vaulted ceilings.

There is an entrance ▶ to the utility room from the existing shelter, saving Paul and Fiona treading mud into the main body of the building.

Fact File costs as of Febuary 2002

NAME: Paul Sargeantson and Fiona Elliott

PROFESSION: Fencing contractor and farm secretary

AREA: Oxfordshire

HOUSE TYPE: Three bed early Georgian style farmhouse

HOUSE SIZE: 198m[2]

BUILD ROUTE: Self as main contractor

CONSTRUCTION: Brick and block

WARRANTY: Zurich

SAP RATING: 89

FINANCE: £65,000 mortgage from Norwich and Peterborough

BUILD TIME: Sept '95 – Mar '97

LAND COST: £65,000

BUILD COST: £85,000

TOTAL COST: £150,000	70%
HOUSE VALUE: £500,000	COST SAVING
COST/m[2]: £429	

Cost Breakdown:

Services and fees:	£1,500
Labour:	£20,000
Bricks, blocks, ready-mixed concrete:	£13,500
Roof tiles:	£3,500
Attic trusses:	£1,400
Joinery:	£7,000
Klargester sewage disposal	£3,800
Glazing:	£1,500
Plumbing:	£6,000
Electrics:	£4,000
Stone floor in hall:	£1,800
Kitchen units and wooden floor	£6,500
Alpha cooker/boiler:	£4,500
Miscellaneous	£10,000
TOTAL	**£85,000**

DIY Rooftiling

Mark Maddocks and his wife Sandra decided to take on the roof tiling of their new home to help save money. We find out if it was as tough as it looks.

Running the family tool and plant hire business gives Mark Maddocks quite a head start when it comes to building work and selecting tradesmen to employ. Nevertheless, when he and Sandra bought the family home from his mother for £100,000, they wanted to get involved with as much hands on experience as they could manage when it came to completely reorganising and modernising the house.

In the first stage of restructuring, Mark's father added a large, flat roofed extension to the rear as well as a double garage. Phase two, which will take the value to £175,000, will involve moving the kitchen to the front of the building, constructing a new dining room, adding a lounge extension to the rear and demolishing the old garage. However, the most eye catching aspect of the work is the roof tiling and that's what we wanted to talk to him about.

Why did you choose to use plain tiles when the two new houses next door have used a cheap interlocking tile?

Looks — this is a traditional house in a beauty spot and I thought that it deserved to have the right roof. It was more expensive but we're very pleased with the result. I would have preferred to go one better and use plain clay tiles — the big house at the top of the hill utilised second hand, plain clay tiles and I've always admired that — but it was just too expensive in the end. We chose Redland Rustic Red tiles with terracotta uni-angle ridge tiles and finials and I'm very pleased with the result that we have achieved.

Doing things yourself means that you can get things just right. I didn't want holes in the felt so we took extra care with that. A friend showed us how to set the battens out and gauge them up the roof — we've got a 100mm gauge, so that's a lot of battening. I can tell you that by the end our knees, heels and calves really ached. We worked from the bottom up and it was important to get things just right as we came into the valleys.

You could have used a lead or even a fibre glass valley, of course.

I could have done but I wouldn't have been as happy. I think the valley tiles set it off beautifully. We did have to use lead in the secret valley at the back, however. The flat roofed extension ran the whole width of the house — if that had been one roof it would have towered above the 'main' roof — so we split it into two pitches with a valley in between.

I know people don't like these and feel that such a secret valley is a recipe for future trouble but really, as long as we make sure that it's kept clear and that the outlet doesn't block, it should be fine. We used the heaviest grade lead for that and laid it with two 100mm steps, making sure that it was dressed well up the roof on the lay boards.

As it was an older house, did you have any problems with the roof not being exactly square?

Yes — and not just on the older bits. The newer extension bowed out a little and we had to jiggle things so that it all lined up. We tiled in from the verges, where we used tiles and halves, and back from the valley tiles — we had to carefully gauge the tiles along the batten to avoid too many cuts. On the main roof we just made adjustments from the fascia upwards, so that we were parallel by the time we got to the ridge. Once again, we carefully gauged things across the roof to avoid cuts. You just close up or separate by a millimetre at a time across the roof — that cancels out most of the discrepancies.

You certainly don't want one of those large angle grinders up there. Loading out is most of the physical work, really. We saved a lot of trouble by getting a machine to lift the pallets onto the especially strengthened scaffold and then loaded out the roof from there. Even so, it was still hard work.

This is a high exposure area and we've nailed every third row and all verge and eaves tiles. By doing things ourselves we've made sure that it was done right — it's the same with the pointing. I've seen so many roofs where the mortar has all cracked within 12 months. We used a coloured mortar and I did it very slowly and carefully, making sure that I got a good joint between it, the undercloak and the tile. I'm going to coat it with a silicone damp proofing material now it's fully set, which will keep the damp out and avoid frost damage.

One thing we did have to check was the roof timbers on the original house. It's vital to make sure that the timbers are sufficient to take the heavier weight. ∎

"You certainly don't want one of those large angle grinders up there. Loading out is most of the physical work really…"

DIY self-builders Toby and Tanya Sherwin have built a fantastic family home in Essex that is worth more than twice what it has cost them.

Words: **Mark Brinkley**   Photography: **Jeremy Pembrey**

Century Moon sits on an unmade road on a former plotlands site in Leigh-on-Sea in Essex. As recently as 1998, there was no development along the road bar a few bungalows dating from the 1930s. Then Rochford District Council saw fit to move its development boundaries and within the space of four years the road has sprouted dozens of large detached houses and scarcely a vacant plot remains. Toby and Tanya Sherwin were one of the first families to build here and because they got in early and built very cheaply, they have made a spectacular return.

Above all else, their project was a family affair. Toby's father David is a well known and successful local housebuilder who is now in semi-retirement and is in the happy position of being able to look around for projects to keep him busy. Whilst Toby's two brothers have worked as builders, Toby himself showed no interest in construction until taking on this self-build. "I had started out life as an actor and Tanya had been a dancer," says Toby. "Now I work as a London taxi driver, starting work at 3pm every day and getting back here after midnight. It had never occurred to me to work with my Dad before this but it has been a really enjoyable experience."

Certainly having a father with plenty of time on his hands, versed in the customs of the building trade, made

for a particularly smooth project. David used his considerable experience to nail down bargain after bargain from suppliers and called on favours from subcontractors, many of whom he has worked with all his life. Toby worked on the building every day from 8 a.m. until he went off in his taxi in the afternoon and Tanya supplied a huge amount of artistic input, designing the lighting scheme and various pieces of furniture.

Their self-build story started when they found the plot while they were walking around the neighbourhood. It had a handwritten For Sale sign on it and an asking price of just £60,000, which looked cheap even in 1998 — today plots in this road go for more than double this price. The problem was that this was an unadopted road with no mains drainage and the council sewer was over 150m away. David says, "There was some talk of a local builder putting in a private sewer and charging people to connect to it but we were worried in might never happen. So we came up with the idea of putting in a pumping station and taking the waste to the municipal sewer. We chose a Sarlin Pumping Station — not the cheapest, but we thought it looked like the most reliable. One of the problems to overcome was to run the 2 inch pipework all the way up the road and onto the next street. We chose to do it one ▶

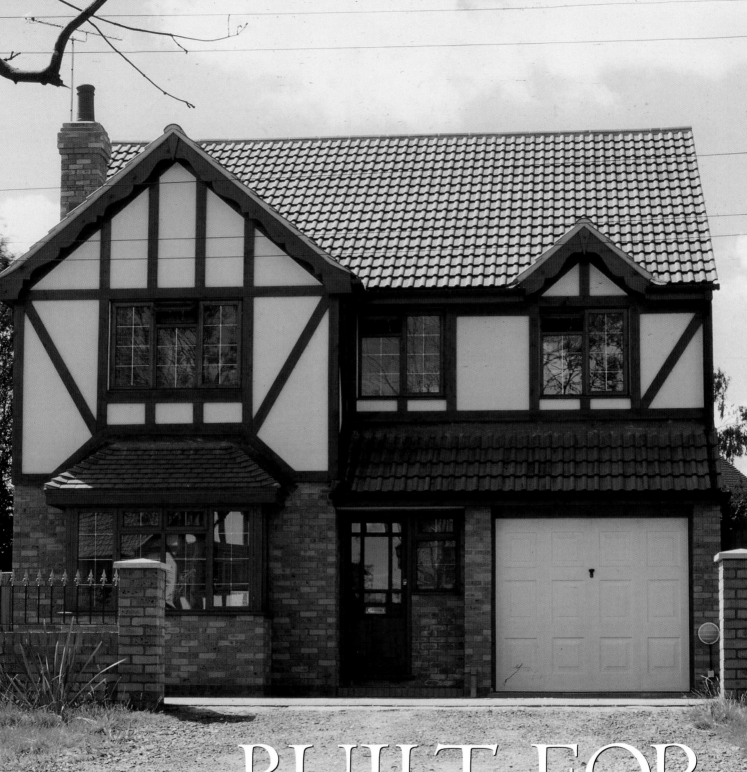

BUILT FOR JUST £84,000!

DIY self-builders save a
fortune on their dream home

The Sherwins ▶ have continued the same quarry tile flooring used in the kitchen into the family living area and conservatory in order to unite them as a single open plan living space.

Sunday morning when the traffic was light, digging two feet deep, unrolling the pipe and filling in again behind, but we did it."

Before they even got this far, they had to sell their existing house and arrange a temporary stay with Tanya's parents. The plans were worked out between the family and one of David's contacts drew them up for planning approval and building regulations. Interestingly, David only agreed to help with the project if he could design the street elevation of the house himself.

"Having been a builder for many years," he says, "I reckon I have a pretty good idea about what makes a house sell and what doesn't, and to my way of thinking

> "We chose to [lay the wastepipe] one Sunday when the traffic was light… it took us all day, but we did it."

The use of attic ▶ trusses has allowed the roofspace to be converted easily into a combined bedroom and playroom for the boys.

it's got to look right from the front kerb. I thought, if ever they have to sell it, it will sell much more easily. I wasn't too bothered about what they did inside and out the back."

In fact there is something of a generational clash of styles at work here because the front elevation is half timbered with decorated barge boards, which fits in well with the rest of the emerging streetscape. But internally, the ground floor layout tends towards open plan and the decoration is clean and modern. Period detailing has been eschewed entirely, with plain skirtings and tiled floors wherever possible.

As might be expected with such experience in the family, the build of the house proceeded remarkably smoothly. Ground was broken in October 1998 and they moved in just eight months later. Toby worked on the house every morning while David organised the subcontractors and busied himself nailing down bargains from his suppliers. One way he was able to help was to buy larger quantities than were needed for just the one house. "I even got the building inspector, who I have known for years, to help out," says David. "We took just one day, a Friday, to excavate the foundations. The Inspector popped round to see them that evening and that allowed us to pour the concrete on Saturday morning. We got a pump in for the job: it cost £240 but was worth every penny." ▶

The modern kitchen came from
Magnet Joinery (01245 262321). The
high quality specification includes
low voltage spotlights throughout.

The conservatory and attic conversion were both additions to the original planning application and help make maximum use of the site.

Just about the only major problem they had was with plasterers. "Plasterers — they are the worst," Toby grins. "We went through three sets before we finished. The first lot just left us one day when they heard about a bigger job down the road. The second just disappeared."

The house construction is brick and block — David has never built any other way — but it does include one major first for him, the use of attic trusses in order to get usable space in the loft. "These attic trusses," he says, "really do seem to be a great idea. They are simple and quick to erect, although you do need a crane on site, and the extra space they give you really opens up a new dimension." The two boys, Joshua and Oscar, share the loftspace, which doubles as a bedroom and extra large playroom.

"The whole thing has been a fantastic experience for us," says Toby. "I've really enjoyed the building side of it, much more than I expected. But perhaps the greatest thing for me is that its brought me and my Dad much closer." Tanya agrees. "It's strange," she says. "They never used to be so close. Now they are best mates!" ∎

Fact File costs as of January 2002

NAME: Toby and Tanya Sherwin

PROFESSIONS: Taxi Driver and housewife

AREA: Essex

HOUSE TYPE: Four bedrooms plus two in loft

HOUSE SIZE: 200m²

BUILD ROUTE: Project managed plus subcontractors

CONSTRUCTION: Brick and block

WARRANTY: NHBC

FINANCE: Private

BUILD TIME: Oct '98 — June '99

LAND COST: £60,000

BUILD COST: £85,000

TOTAL COST: £145,000

CURRENT VALUE: £300,000

COST/m²: £425

52% COST SAVING

First Floor

The downstairs layout is fairly open plan, while the first floor has four bedrooms, with the fifth being in the loftspace (NOT SHOWN).

Useful Contacts

Design and build — David Sherwin Construction: 01268 565647

Building Materials — Canvey Island Supply Co: 01268 696666

Kitchens, doors, windows — Magnet Joinery: 01245 262321

Heating — Taymour Heating: 01268 752940

Tiles — Pitsea Tiles: 01268 552222

Roofing — Seeco Roofing: 01702 480303

Floors — Milbank Floors (Beam and Block floor): 01787 223931

Sewerage — Grundfos Sarlin Pump: 01525 850000

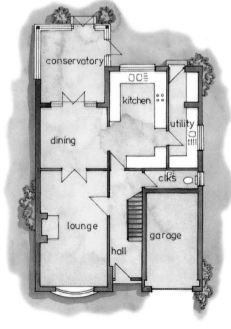

Ground Floor

DIY Electrics & Plumbing

Mick Farrier bought a run down terraced house with a view to either keeping it or letting it out. David Snell discovers how he took on, amongst other things, the electrics and plumbing.

When he took early retirement from a hectic job as an aircraft engineer, Mick Farrier thought, like many others, that the most sensible way to invest his lump sum was to purchase an old terraced house in Derby and renovate it with a view to either keeping it on or letting it out.

The house cost him £31,000 and he has spent the last six months alone in it day after day, stripping it out and refurbishing it to the point where it is now valued at £40,000. He has spent no more than £3,000 on materials and the real cost of what he put into the project is his own time. Most of the work has been cosmetic: things like new kitchen units, bathroom suites and general redecoration. To bring a house like this into the modern age, however, requires the installation of modern plumbing and central heating and whilst doing that he decided to upgrade the electrics.

What was wrong with the electrics?

Not that much really. In fact there was a modern consumer unit and RCD trip. The problem was that in a three bedroom house there was a total of four power points and that's simply not enough. For our purposes you need at least four in each room so I had to install two new ring mains. The lighting was fine but I also decided to put TV aerials and telephone sockets in each room and as a result quite a few of the boards upstairs had to come up. With the difficulty of routing everything through an old house it's often meant that I've had to approach points from strange directions but wherever possible I've tried to keep runs vertical to the outlets.

Did you have trouble getting the boards up in an old house?

No. Surprisingly, the boards weren't tongued and grooved so it was easy to lift them one at a time. I bought a really great tool in the States called a Stanley Wonderbar. It's a bit like a short and flattened wrecking bar or jemmy and you can slip the end in between the boards and get them up without damaging them. I always screw rather than nail the boards back down. It means they don't squeak and the process is reversible.

But surely you did not drill through the old joists for the central heating?

In places, yes, although with a house of this type the floorboards are remarkably thin, barely 150mm but spaced quite closely and if you took too much out of them you'd weaken them to an unacceptable degree. For the most part I've opted for surface mounting behind ducting. In places where I've dropped to radiators it is behind proprietary sheathing, but in other places where there are main runs, I've battened out and boarded. In fact with the bathroom and kitchen downstairs at the back of the house, the water and gas supplies had to come right through the house and I've channelled them behind a double layer of skirting.

Were you tempted to use plastic plumbing?

Not really, even though it might have been easier to get to otherwise inaccessible places. I'm used to using copper and as an ex aircraft engineer, I can't get it out of my head that plastic is a material that degrades. What are the first things that crack up in your motor car? Of course the supply pipe itself is the blue alkathene. The water board operate a policy whereby if you take all the lead piping out, they'll do the same for their supply. Here everything, even the wastes, were lead. I'm not a complete Luddite and I've used flexible tap connectors and gone for a gas fired combination boiler. I like the boiler I've used. It's a

Halstead 80 from Wickes and here it's the obvious answer because if it's not used it recycles itself every day and runs for about five minutes. Things like pumps stick if they're not opened from time to time, they need to be operated. With just one bathroom and a kitchen sink a combination boiler is ideal and in fact it's over capacity that's the problem.

I've had to restrict the gates to the sinks and taps so as not to rob the shower and I'm going to have to set the boiler down to about half of its output as it's too big for this house.

What about commissioning?

With the electrics, no problem. I've tested it all out and I was only wiring from an existing consumer unit. I've had to read the IEEE guide so that I've got the correct cross bonding; with the boiler, I will have to get a Corgi registered plumber in to check out the system and fire it up. With this boiler it's possible to have water in the system without firing up as the boiler is separate and simply hangs over the expansion vessel. That means that I could fill up the system so I've flushed it through and tested out at mains pressure. ∎

"I always screw rather than nail the boards back down. It means they don't squeak..."

Past Made Present

Russell and Janet Robson have built an authentic looking cottage from scratch for just £120,000 thanks to their innovative approach to materials.

Words:
Clive Fewins

Photography:
Nigel Rigden

From the look of the windows and roof levels in Russell and Janet Robson's cottage style home in a Dorset village, you would think it had been built over several periods. The garage, with its clay-tiled roof with a bedroom above, looks like a later addition to the thatched building, while the more rustic weatherboarded southern end with its steeply hipped gable looks like an agricultural building that has been incorporated into the main house. Only on close inspection does it become apparent that it is a new build; in fact Russell, a house designer and conversion specialist, and his wife Janet only moved in three years ago. Only the new local stone gives the game away. And, as Russell points out, this will weather in a few years.

Russell has designed many homes in England and overseas but this is his first complete self-build. "We were living in nearby Broadwindsor when we discovered this plot and thought it ideal for a self-build for our retirement," Russell says. "We were drawn to it because it is in a glorious position on the edge of the village with wonderful views to open country across the rooftops. It was one of three adjacent plots and faces south. Although it is only a quarter of an acre and the garden is too small for us really – previously we had 12 acres – you have to make some compromises for a site of this quality."

**The house ▶
was designed in
different styles to
create the illusion
of an old building
that had evolved
over the
centuries.**

Building a traditional cottage from scratch

The inglenook ▶ fireplace in the lounge was aged by lighting an open fire in it as soon as it was built.

There had been outline planning consent for a new dwelling on the site for many years. The Robsons encountered little difficulty with the detailed planning application, having realised that with a sensitive site in the heart of the conservation area, in a picture postcard village, something in a very traditional style was likely to raise few objections.

"The plan was to produce a cottage style home that would be modern but looked old and that would be easy on maintenance."

"Only a new 'old' house could look right in a village like this, where there is a preponderance of stone and thatch," Russell says. "The plan was to produce a cottage style home that would be modern but looked old and that would be easy on maintenance."

The thatch is the biggest factor in creating the illusion of age. The dormer to the south of the west-facing front elevation, with its sloping roof leading right up to the thatched ridge, appears to be a possible later insert. So does the low eaves window above the porch, while the thatched hipped end over the front stone projection gives more than a hint of great age.

The ground floor window in this part of the building is a genuine period piece of fine local stone, a gift from a friend who renovated properties. Russell added a matching hood-mould over the top that he had cast in a local

workshop and inserted a 1950s style metal framed Crittall window that he double glazed himself.

"It pained me to have to have a new steel window frame made to measure to fit inside the stone casing but as the surround was free and it was a hopeless task to try and find one at a reclamation yard, I had to pay up," says Russell. "I knew it was the only way the window would look right in that position because wooden casements would be far too thick in such a narrow space."

Perhaps surprisingly, Russell chose American-made Andersen windows for most of the house. "They suited the design perfectly; as well as being very well made and 'tight', they are extremely secure," he says. "We decided the 'Terratone' exterior colour fitted in well with what we had in mind." They are made from timber encased in coloured vinyl on the exterior and so are designed for low maintenance.

The only drawback was that the nine Andersen windows they required would cost nearly £8,000 and Russell was determined to keep to his budget of a maximum £500/m². "Our policy was to spend money on the important things, and windows that would not rot and would need very little maintenance were high on the list," says Russell. "We found that the Andersen range came in all the shapes and sizes we wanted. This meant, however, that we had to save money in other ways."

One way the Robsons did this was to use two far cheaper sliding patio doors from a local supplier (now no longer trading) on the south and east elevations facing the ▶

The rear ▶ elevation is clad in local stone and horizontal weatherboarding in macrocarpa.

two sections of garden. Another saving was made by using reclaimed interlocking clay tiles rather than thatch on the wing over the garage. Russell was reluctant to do this but Janet loves it. "I think it makes for a good contrast at the front," she says.

Other savings were also made by using reclaimed materials, namely the wealth of huge oak beams in the downstairs ceiling – a gift from a house restorer friend – which Russell cunningly managed to drop to 2.1m while still conforming to the Building Regulations.

"They 'aged' the inglenook, in which they have installed a gas coal effect stove by lighting a large fire in the structure before the roof or ceiling were built…"

Over the inglenook fireplace in the sitting room – which is constructed from reclaimed bricks – they have used a large beam left over that came from a conversion job they undertook when they lived in a watermill many years ago. They 'aged' the inglenook, in which they have installed a gas coal effect stove, by lighting a fire in the structure before the roof or ceiling was constructed, allowing it to blaze away for several hours. "Some brickies working nearby who saw it thought we were crazy when they realised what we were doing, but the trick worked perfectly," Russell says.

Fact File costs as of April 2002

NAMES: Russell and Janet Robson

PROFESSIONS: Landlords and house designer

AREA: South-west Dorset

HOUSE TYPE: Five bedroom detached with thatched roof

HOUSE SIZE: 240m²

BUILD ROUTE: Selves as main contractors

CONSTRUCTION: Inner leaf of blockwork. Cladding of stone and weatherboarding

WARRANTY: Zurich

SAP RATING: 100

FINANCE: Private

BUILD TIME: Eight months

LAND COST: £80,000

BUILD COST: £120,000

TOTAL COST: £200,000

CURRENT VALUE: £400,000

COST/m²: £500

50% COST SAVING

Cost Breakdown:

Groundworks:	£11,000
Shell:	£24,000
Windows:	£8,000
Oak doors:	£2,000
Roof timbers and tiles:	£9,000
Thatch:	£8,000
Plumbing:	£4,000
Joinery:	£3,500
Plastering	£5,000
Electrics:	£8,000
Underfloor heating:	£9,000
Bathroom and sanitaryware:	£2,500
Kitchen:	£600
Scaffolding:	£3,000
Insulation:	£2,000
Timber and quarry tiles for flooring	£3,000
Labour and sundries:	£17,500
TOTAL	**£120,100**

From the friend who gave them the oak beams and the mullioned stone window, Tom Gibbs, they also acquired their sturdy panelled pine front door. "It was on an outbuilding of his when I first saw it," Russell says. "It was filthy and painted a ghastly colour but I could see it was very solid, had two vertical glass panels and was three feet wide — just what we wanted for a front door. Tom took it off and made me a gift of it."

The Robsons also made savings on the kitchen by keeping to an 'unfitted' look. They bought a painted Welsh

FLOORPLAN: The roofspace over the garage has been used to provide a guest bedroom with en suite facilities.

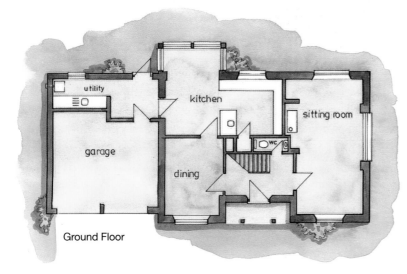

First Floor

Ground Floor

dresser and a glass cabinet plus a few old pine pieces from local junk shops. "It was hard work finding the right pieces but we think the finished effect is very good," Janet says. The final price tag, including the Belfast sink, was £600.

Another saving that paid off was the hall floor. It came from a fallen chestnut tree Russell spotted in the field of a local landowner. Russell bought it, had it planked, and got his team to lay the boards green on timber joists. As expected, the planks have shrunk and opened up to produce a pleasantly aged effect.

> "Another saving that paid off was the hall floor. It came from a fallen chestnut tree Russell spotted in the field…"

Outside, the timber fleur-de-lys finial over the front porch was originally a pew end in a redundant church. It had been in Russell's store shed for many years. The weatherboarding on the south-facing 'rustic' wing is macrocarpa, an American timber with a lovely silver hue that weathers as well as cedar, needs no treatment and is much cheaper than oak.

One feature they were not prepared to compromise on was the underfloor heating, which they installed on both floors. "The house is very warm and cosy in winter," says Russell, "helped by the thatch and high levels of insulation in the walls and floor. It is also easy to maintain and we think it looks just right in its setting. It is exactly the sort of house I have always wanted to build for the two of us." ■

Useful Contacts

Designer – Russell Robson:	01308 459248
Bricklayer – Owen Crabb:	0370 923856
Plasterer – Eugene Crabb:	01308 427678
Electrician – Tim Noyes:	01308 863252
Plumbing and heating – Dave Murley:	01308 424861
Carpenters – Barry Clare:	01308 425539
Duncan Jones:	01308 458006
Thatcher – Dave Simmonds:	01297 489800
Main Windows – Andersen:	01283 511122
Metal Windows – Crittall:	01376 324106
Timber – Forest and Tree Care:	01308 456218
Travis Perkins:	01308 422351
Reclaimed Bricks – Jewsons:	01308 423651
Reclaimed clay roofing – Yeovil Roofing:	01935 421326
Stone cladding – Monument:	01458 274587
Reconstituted stone sills and window hood – Mill Lane Cast Concrete:	01460 74415
Kitchen quarry tiles – County Tile warehouse:	01305 261400

DIY Plastering

Pauline Toynbee saved £1,000s on her barn conversion by doing all of the plastering by herself – a task she took on because her builder couldn't give her the effect she wanted.

▲ Pauline plasters the walls of the barn's roofspace — it may well yield another bedroom. "I wanted it to look rough," she says, "but I didn't want it to look as if it had been deliberately distressed."

Pauline Toynbee and her husband Philip have bought a variety of houses to do up and sell. But they have always wanted to do a barn conversion and when the opportunity came up to buy a semi derelict barn and stockyard on the edge of the South Downs, they jumped at the chance.

The barn cost them £137,000. It is not a very big building – in fact its ground floor is probably no more than 100m² – but it will make a very comfortable home and when it is finished there will be two bedrooms on the ground floor with the possibility of a further one in the roof.

When we spoke to them in September 2001 they had spent £37,000 so far on the conversion work and they reckoned that by the time they finished, assuming they didn't go too mad back and putting the second coat on. If it went on the way I wanted then I would leave it alone but sometimes I would have to fiddle with it to get it right. I left in all of the nicer drag marks. They have an authentic rusticity.

We have tried very hard to achieve good U-values. On the roof and the sloping ceilings we have got 70mm of Celotex foil backed rigid urethane insulation. We painted all of the plasterboard first and put it up on top of the rafters, white side down. It is not easy painting 60 sheets of plasterboard on an open building site — but we did it. After that there is a vapour barrier and then the insulation with counter battens fixed through all that to the rafters in order to take the tiling battens. Painting the plasterboard first means that we don't now

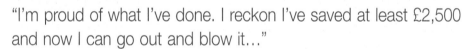

"I'm proud of what I've done. I reckon I've saved at least £2,500 and now I can go out and blow it…"

on fittings and fixtures, they'd be up at around the £60,000 mark, making a total of £197,000 to set against a value of around £250,000.

Between the two of them, and with some help from their son Christian, Pauline and Philip are mixing the use of DIY and subcontracted labour but what we wanted to talk to Pauline about was the fact that she has undertaken the plastering herself, saving around £2,500.

What possessed you to take on the plastering? I wasn't going to do it at first but I couldn't get what I wanted from the builder. I wanted it to look rough – as if it had been there a while – with all the natural knocks and blemishes, but I didn't want it to look as if it had been deliberately distressed.

You're a potter. Did that come in handy? It meant I already had the knowledge that if you didn't get it right or like it, you could always scrape it off and start again. I used Carlite Bonding in two coats. I would put one on and then go away and let it firm up before coming

have to cut in the paintwork to the beams and all we have to do is tape and fill the joints, so all that hard work paid off.

We used the same principle for the ground floor ceiling and painted the chipboard decking before we put it down. I like the fact that we have got the full depth of the beams to the roof and the first floor showing. If we opt for underfloor central heating to the upper part we will lose part of that so we are veering towards using radiators up there.

What about the walls? The builder waterproof rendered the inside of the stone walls. We fixed 28mm Celotex insulation sheets vertically and have held them against the wall with battens. We have used 12mm ply for those because it allows us to have a wider batten and it means that the batten can be quite thin without the danger of it splitting. Before tacking the plasterboard to the battens we have taped up and sealed the joints in the insulation with insulating tape. Around the exposed beams and where the joists run into the wall we have been careful not to leave any gaps in the insulation and create cold spots. Where there is a gap we have filled it with offcuts and as time has gone on we've become experts at cutting plasterboard and getting it right. At the top the wall slopes out to the plate leaving a ledge. I have cut the plasterboard to that and put insulation on the top of the wall before plastering it in. Because of the waterproof render we have also had to use plastic electrical boxes as there is no fixing through to the wall.

In retrospect, would you have done anything differently? No. I wouldn't have been happy if I hadn't done the plastering myself and as I took it over, I'm pleased with how it's turned out. There is one corner in the lounge, for example, that the builder started and it is sharp. I wanted rounded corners and edges, so I cut the plasterboard back at the angles and created a hard corner of plaster that I rounded off to look natural. I reckon that by doing it that way I've got a harder wearing corner anyway.

I'm proud of what I've done. I reckon I've saved at least £2,500 and now that I've saved all that money, I can go out and blow it on something special or a kitchen that's a little bit better. ■

THE HOUSE

Ultra low-energy self-build

Dave and Ingun Roberts have built a remarkable low-cost, low-maintenance, low-energy family house on Scotland's north east coast.

Words and Photography: **Fiona Cameron**

WITHOUT HEATING

The downside of choosing a very innovative design for your home is that it can seem as if you're living in the middle of an experiment. That's a little how the Roberts family of Aberdeen have felt since they moved into their new house just before Christmas 2000 — there's been a lot of interest from the media and a local university's carrying out a year-long monitoring project. However, on balance Dave and Ingun Roberts feel it's well worth it.

One of the last places you'd expect anyone to deliberately choose a house without heating is Scotland's cold shoulder — the north east coast. Yet that's exactly what Dave and Ingun specified for their family's new home — no central heating — plus minimal maintenance routines, and an affordable price.

Although zero-energy homes are not a new idea, many of the insulation and energy saving ideas adopted in the past have made such homes very expensive to build — the ►

"Dave reckons the total energy bill for space heating will be substantially less than £100 over the year."

solar panels designed to raise the ambient temperature of domestic hot water to around 30°C. A high proportion of glazing in the front wall and porch area (south facing) serves as a heat collecting area, while glazing has been kept to a minimum on the north, east and west walls. The design makes use of a familiar local tradition — the back door is intended to be the one in normal everyday use.

The use of I-beams in the construction has allowed the insertion of much thicker than standard insulation in the walls with no additional structural costs. 300mm of Warmcell (a recycled newspaper product treated with inorganic salts to render it fire resistant) has been used; there is 200mm of rigid polystyrene under the solid concrete floor (which also acts as a heat mass) and a further 450mm of Warmcell in the roof. All windows are triple-glazed krypton filled units using low-E glass. A mechanical ventilation system with heat recovery ensures ventilation is adequate whilst almost no heat is wasted.

The interior layout is also unusual — the use of I-beams means there is far more usable space on the upper floor, as well as minimal circulation space downstairs. All rooms open off the central living area and upstairs gallery, allowing not only maximum productive use of floor space but

Roberts were determined to stick to a strict budget in terms of build costs. They had already purchased a site on the outskirts of a city suburb and found an architect who could fulfil these requirements right on their doorstep. Some four years ago, Aberdeen's Robert Gordon University ran a research project on affordable rural housing prototypes. One of the staff members most closely involved was architect Gokay Deveci.

The Roberts had experienced problems with finding an architect who could design a house which met their requirements. They contacted Deveci and a short time later their new home was well on the way. Because local planners are enthusiastic about energy conservation, there were no problems in securing planning permission for the five bedroom home, despite the fact that the house differs radically from most of its traditionally built neighbours.

All of the walls are finished in locally sourced larch cladding and the roofing material chosen was one widespread throughout Eastern Scotland — red pantiles (though these come from Yorkshire!). The roof incorporates

All the walls are finished in locally sourced larch cladding, from Cardiner & Sons (01224 248800).

also efficient heat circulation. The double height central living area, coupled with the high proportion of glazing, gives a spacious feel to the 130m² house.

Although a wood burning stove was included as a focal point for the living area, in theory, the body heat of the occupants should mean the internal temperature never falls below 14°C, even in the depths of a Scottish winter.

The Roberts family — Dave, Ingun and their three children — moved in just before Christmas 2000 and Dave says they've used the wood burner for no more than an hour or two on the very coldest days of winter. He admits they've broken the rules more than a few times too — opening the front door more than was intended during the settling-in phase, for instance.

However, tests conducted over a three day period in January showed temperatures which never fell below 17°C, even without heating. Dave reckons the total energy bill for space heating will be substantially less than £100 over the year. He smiles ruefully as he recollects, "When we were living in a mobile home on site while the house was built, our electric bills alone were around £150 a month!"

So much for the energy efficiency — what about the Roberts' stipulation that build and maintenance costs should be low? Gokay Deveci reckons that the build cost (just over £57,000, giving a cost per m² of £435) reflects a saving of more than 20% on the cost of a similar spec built house of traditional construction. The house took only sixteen weeks from foundations to completion.

Although it's unusual to see Scottish houses completely clad in wood, the Roberts have had relatively few problems with either their insurers or with a mortgage. Maintenance costs on the locally sourced larch cladding should be virtually nil. The BMI recommend inspection and general repair (if necessary) every fifteen years and the life expectancy of the cladding is about sixty years. Deveci reckons that re-cladding could be done after that time for ▶

Large areas of glazing on the south side acts as a form of heat collector while there is significantly less glass on the colder north side.

"The house took only sixteen weeks to build, from foundations to completion…"

Useful Contacts

Architect — Gokay Deveci:
01224 263714

I-Beams — Fillcrete (Masonite):
01482 233405

Insulation — Warmcell: 01482 233405

Windows & Glazing — Nor-Dan by Aberdeen Windows and Doors Systems Ltd: 01224 633174

Rooflights — The Velux Company Ltd:
01592 772211

Solar Water Heating System — Solar panels from AES Solar Systems:
01309 676911

Stainless steel stove pipe — Selkirk, supplied by Northern Heating Supplies:
01224 663322

Rooftiles — Sandtoft Country Pantiles from Sandtoft Roof Tiles Ltd:
01427 871200

Heat recovering mechanical vents — Baxi s-24 low voltage mechanical fans:
08706 060780

Larch cladding — Local Scottish larch from Cordiner & Sons: 01224 248800

Breather membrane — Tyvek by Klober Ltd: 01934 853224

Boarding — 9.5mm Panelvent by Fillcrete: 01482 233405

Internal wood finish — Auro organic paints by Auro Organic Paint Supplies Ltd: 01799 543077

Internal wall paint finish — Ecos Emulsion by Lakeland Paints:
01524 852371

The large overhang of the roof helps to protect the timber walls from rainfall. Note the solar panels from AES Systems (01309 676911).

"It was plain sailing as far as receiving planning was concerned, because Aberdeen city planners are enthusiastic about energy conservation."

Fact File costs as of May 2001

NAME: Dave and Ingun Roberts

PROFESSION: Commercial manager

AREA: Aberdeen

HOUSE TYPE: 4/5 bedroom detached

HOUSE SIZE: 127m^2

BUILD ROUTE: Main contractor

CONSTRUCTION: I-beam post and beam structure with larch cladding

SAP RATING: 120

FINANCE: Mortgage

BUILD TIME: Four months

LAND COST: est £40,000

BUILD COST: £57,269

TOTAL COST: £97,269

HOUSE VALUE: £110,000

COST/M^2: £450

12% COST SAVING

The ground floor has minimal circulation space — the savings have gone into a dramatic double height area at the entrance.

the equivalent of £1,500 at today's prices. He admits that the concept might need revision if applied in the higher-rainfall climate of the west of Scotland.

What were the problems? It was plain sailing as far as receiving planning was concerned, because Aberdeen city planners are enthusiastic about energy conservation. In other areas, this stage of the process can be more of an obstacle to overcome. Indeed, the only matter that held up the start of building was the problem of drainage connection.

How much potential has this type of construction for other self-build projects? Virtually limitless, according to Gokay Deveci. He would like to see the house the Roberts built become the norm for new housing all over the country. He is enthusiastic about the use of sustainable materials but even more so about the energy savings that could be achieved if all the four and a half million homes projected as being needed in the UK by 2016 were built on zero heating principles. The annual fuel bill savings would be £921 million. ∎

Ground Floor

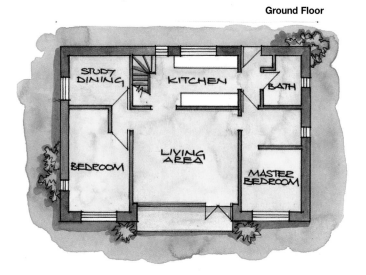

First Floor

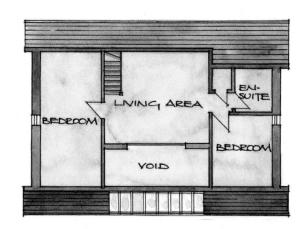

46

DIY Electrics

Frank and Emma McCarthy have saved a fortune building their new home in Wales, largely by doing much of the work on a DIY basis. We asked Frank what it was like doing his own electrics.

▲ Putting your own electrics into a brand new home involves an awful lot of planning in addition to physical labour.

Frank and Emma McCarthy upped sticks and moved from London so that their children could grow up in Wales, where they bought a plot for £55,000 and camped out with Emma's parents, finally making a start on their new house in April 2000.

The plot they bought would have frightened many people with its daunting slope dictating a multi-level design but they've seen it through and in eight months have built themselves a 325m², five bedroom house. Building costs have added £120,000 and it's valued at £240,000. It hasn't been easy. Emma has held down a full time job while looking after three children under five and Frank has had to live away during the week with his job as a fireman in London. Despite that, they've done a lot themselves, including the electrics.

Did you have any experience as an electrician?

Before I joined the Fire Service, I had trained as an electrician and so, although it was quite a while ago, had that experience to fall back on. Nevertheless, this was a big project to take on in many respects, especially as I was going to have to do it on a part time basis and needed to read up on the latest regulations and make myself aware of the innovations that have taken place.

What was the biggest challenge?

The planning. This house is on three levels, four if you count the loft space, and we've used solid beam and block floors throughout. Now, although the beam and block floors allow you to take the wires wherever you want in the ceiling void between the battens holding the plasterboard and the beams, once you've got them there and the ceilings are up, it's near impossible to get back to them. It's not as if you can just rip up a floorboard because with the ceilings up, the floors screeded and the

UFH in, so much would be ruined. We had to work out where every socket and switch was going to be and had to get it right. We spent hours walking around deciding which way doors would open and where the furniture would go.

Did the beam and block floor make things complicated?

No. As I explained, you can travel anywhere with the wires in the ceiling void. The beams have little galvanised loops on them that you hitch the wires through or to and the space between the underside of the beams and the plasterboard is around 75mm. We've got two separate ring mains for both power and lighting on each floor as each one exceeds the 100m². I just started off in the basement level and worked upwards, following the builders. I opened an account with the local electrical supply company. I just gave myself a name — FMC Electrics — and got all the usual trade discounts.

You don't need to be qualified to do the work because the Board will test out the system before putting the power on and won't do so unless they're satisfied. Anyway, we've got a temporary supply on so that I can test each section as I finish and I bought myself an Installation Residual Tester.

Any bits that you found hard?

I'm a bit shy of the boiler. I understand it all but want a plumber here when I finally wire up and run it — there are so many pumps running off thermostats and line valves for the underfloor central heating. The only mistake I know I've

made is to leave the wires out for one manifold zone valve in the basement. I'll have to pick up the supply from somewhere else, probably a lighting circuit. I was also disappointed with the requirements of the new Part M Building Regs for special needs, making us put the sockets, for us, too high and the switches too low. Now the children will be able to fiddle with the switches.

Any tips for other DIY self-builders?

Don't be hassled. Take your time to think things out. One tradesman was hurrying me and I nearly made a big mistake. The staircase splits at the first landing and then goes two ways to the gallery. I nearly wired it up for three way switching rather than the four it needs because I was being rushed. Again, in the utility room, I had to take the time to think about the freezer and I felt that it should be on a radial. Modern RCDs trip out so easily and I decided it should be on its own. I would also recommend low voltage lighting: we have used 12V downlighters in the hall, galleries and staircases. The effect is marvellous and they are easy to install. ■

"I was disappointed with the new Part M Regulations making us put the sockets, for us, too high and the switches too low"

Tim and Mairi Turner have built a vernacular style home in reclaimed stone and slate that already looks as if it has stood in its setting for years.

Words:
Tim Turner

Photography:
Douglas Gibb

"We decided the best way for us to afford a house in the countryside was if we built it ourselves," recalls Tim Turner, who together with wife Mairi has built a traditional stone and slate house, tucked into the contour of the landscape, 750ft above sea level, at the foot of the Ochil Hills in Clackmannanshire.

"We heard about the half acre site from a friend," says Tim, "and when we first looked at it in 1990 it had everything we required: fine views of the surrounding hills; it was well away from the main road; the services were adjacent; and from a security point of view there were neighbours nearby. There was even a good pub within walking distance! However, the access road was not very good and for 250m the only thing preventing a 30m sheer drop into the river was a barbed wire fence."

Outline planning permission was granted in 1992 on the basis of replacing a part ruined building on the site, but there were several conditions imposed: the new dwelling was to be built on the roadside, could only be single storey and was to be of vernacular design.

"We would only have wished to build a traditional design, so this was not a problem," explains Tim. "However, a house at the roadside would have restricted the site to an 8m width rather than the 35m at the back and we could not have fitted in the septic tank. As the planning department had just allowed a new two storey building to the rear of the site we thought that this condition could be altered. We ended up employing a planning consultant and in 1993, after a year of letters, we decided to appeal ▶

▼ The proportions of the design – 20ft across at the gables – are typical of the vernacular stone buildings of the area.

48

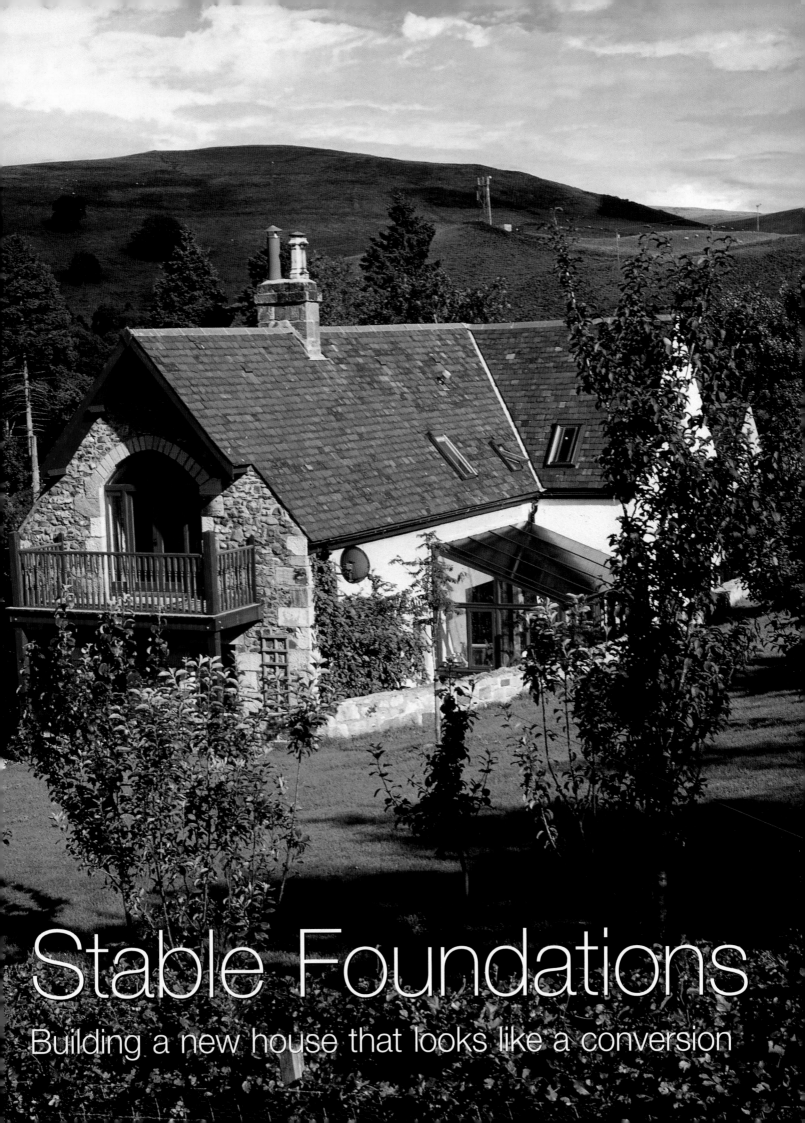

Stable Foundations

Building a new house that looks like a conversion

"The Turners' main objective was to create a house that looked as if it had always been there…"

▲ The kitchen doors and worktops were made from 9" tongue and groove oak boards milled from a tree which Tim had felled himself some years earlier.

to the then Scottish Office. It took a whole year before our appeal could be heard, but after a 20 minute site visit, the inspector was in our favour."

It was not therefore until 1995 that the Turners finally won approval for their design, and even then it came with a requirement from the Highways Department for the shared access road to be upgraded. "At this stage we had reached a fairly low point in our resolve to continue, but designing the house kept us on track," says Tim.

The Turners' main objective was to create a house that looked as if it had always been there. This meant using both local materials – rubble stone walls and slate roof – but also following vernacular design traditions. This included building the house into the contour of the hill to help shield it from the elements, tall narrow windows, arched doorways and external stone steps.

Inside, the house was to have spacious accommodation for guests, a double height lounge with a vaulted ceiling and a minstrels gallery walking out onto a balcony for the views down the glen and of the sunsets.

"We chose a T-shaped floorplan as being the most economic to build and drew up scale drawings of the house and site ourselves," explains Tim. "As we knew exactly ▶

The main ▶ living room is an impressive double height space overlooked by a gallery which leads out the balcony. Internal windows in the master bedroom overlook the room.

"'We chose a T-shape as being the most economic to build and drew up scale drawings ourselves…'"

what we wanted and having not been very impressed with architect's drawings and their practicality, we chose a structural engineer to draw up the plans. This saved on costs as we had to produce structural drawings anyway."

The first stage of the build, in the Autumn of 1995, was to clear the site and build a big retaining wall at the back where the house sits into the hillside. Tim and Mairi were keen to do as much of the work as possible themselves to save on costs. Apart from the plastering and electrics, they managed just about everything. The foundations were dug in spring of 1996. The most cost effective structural solution for building on the hard gravel ground was a simple raft structure. As the access road to the site was too narrow for a ready mixed concrete delivery, Tim had to hand-mix the necessary 20m^3 of concrete himself.

Building the structure of the one and a half storey house up to roofplate level took a whole summer. The walls were

Useful Contacts

General Contractor – Tim Turner:
01259 781270

General materials – Parkhead Building Supplies: 01259 214334

Structural timber and specialist mouldings – Hugh Campbell and sons:
01786 841204.

Reclaimed stone and new cut stone – Tradstocks: 01786 850400

Staircases – Timber components:
01324 717171

Windows – Allanbridge joinery:
01786 446422

Insulation – Clyde Insulation:
01324 613819

Plumbing supplies – Plumbline:
01786 471471

Slates – Travis Perkins: 01324 554111

Range – Aga Rayburn: 01952 642000

Structural engineer – John Ramsbottom: 01786 823331

Electrician – David Peebles:
01738 447591

built using a blockwork inner leaf, with a 50mm insulated cavity and then 250mm stonework on the outside. This unusual wall thickness was necessary to allow the use of the traditional local stone laid as random rubble.

All of the internal walls are 100mm blockwork taken up through to support the A-frame roof structure and to provide internal sound deadening. They also chose blockwork rather than timber framed internal walls because they wanted a traditional hard plastered finish to provide a good base for tiling and fixing.

"We had by this stage found and stored quite a lot of second hand materials from demolition sites, including the gutters and pipes, and the stone lintels, cills and quoins," recalls Tim. "All of the remaining reclaimed lintels and rybat setts came via specialist stone suppliers, Tradstocks, so there were no new materials anywhere on the external face. On the roof we used 15,000 reclaimed Welsh roof slates to match the surrounding buildings. It was very hard to obtain good second hand slate and the wastage was high. It would have been cheaper to use new slate!"

Tim found some beautiful old shellac varnished pine and oak doors that had lain in an outbuilding for 40 years and fitted these throughout. The kitchen worktops and doors are all made from oak, as are the window cills. Tim had felled and planked the timber himself a few years earlier with the intention of using it as flooring, but had decided it was too good for the job. They also had skirting and architrave made to their own design in Scots pine.

"At this stage we installed an oil-fired Rayburn in the kitchen to dry out the house," says Tim. "We stored the finishing timbers in the kitchen to keep them from absorbing moisture." The kitchen range provides core heat whilst the rest of the house is powered by an oil-fired boiler, backed up by a 10kW woodburning stove in the lounge.

With Tim handling so much of the work himself, the Turners were resigned to a lengthy build. However, what they had not foreseen was that the elevation of the site, and the resultant hard frosts, would prevent any masonry work in the winter. Consequently the project took considerably longer than they had expected.

"We hoped the duration of the project would also enable us to spread payment over a long time so that we wouldn't end up with a large loan. We had intended to move in as soon as the house was habitable but with the arrival of a baby, the house really needed finishing quickly and so our mortgage extended."

▲ Mairi and Tim spent weeks driving around abandoned walls collecting the 120 tonnes needed for the external walls.

▶

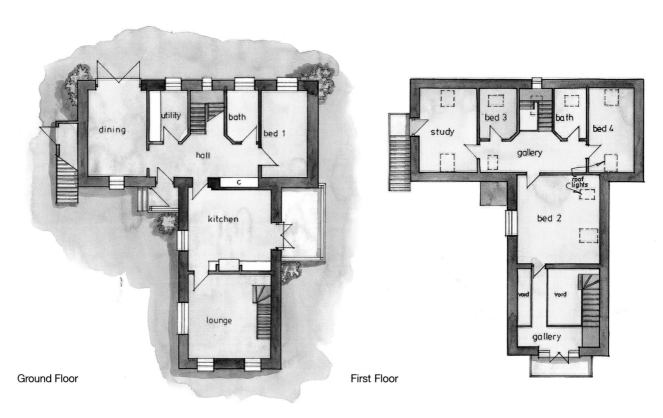

FLOORPLAN: The living room is a double height space overlooked by a first floor gallery. These original drawings show plans for a bridge over the living room linking the master bedroom to the gallery, but this was never constructed.

Ground Floor

First Floor

Fact File costs as of June 2002

NAMES: Tim and Mairi Turner

PROFESSIONS: Stonemason and Administrator

AREA: Clackmannanshire, Scotland

HOUSE TYPE: Four bed detached

HOUSE SIZE: 294m²

BUILD ROUTE: DIY plus subbies

CONSTRUCTION: Cavity walls clad in stone with slate roof

WARRANTY: Engineer's Certificate

FINANCE: Loans: Bank of Scotland

BUILD TIME: Oct '95 – Dec '99

LAND COST: £20,000

BUILD COST: £105,250

TOTAL COST: £125,250

37% COST SAVING

HOUSE VALUE: £200,000

COST/m²: £358

Cost Breakdown:

Groundworks	£11,500
Services	£4,750
Stonework and blocks	£23,000
Roof	£24,500
Plastering	£2,100
Plumbing and heating	£4,400
Electrics	£1,400
Kitchen	£2,500
Rayburn	£2,300
Internal joinery	£12,500
Windows, specialist joinery	£6,000
Conservatory	£3,000
Decorating Tiling	£7,300
TOTAL	**£105,250**

The family finally moved in two days before Christmas 1999. Although there were quite a lot of internal works still to complete, the garden and hedges were by this time quite established, as they had undertaken all of the planting when they first fenced the site.

"In retrospect there are of course a few things that we would change," reflects Tim. "The kitchen and lounge don't really get the morning sun and we feel that the Velux windows are not really suitable facing the prevailing wind and rain. But the balcony works well and the position of the house on the site gives us privacy and shelter from the South Westerly winds.

"One of the nicest things about the house is that we are frequently asked what the building was before we converted it. Having seen so many new houses that looked bare and unsheltered for years after their completion, we are proud of the fact that our home really does already look as if it has been here for many years." ■

DIY Underfloor Heating

The massive cost saving Gordon Wilson enjoyed on his new four bedroom home came about in part thanks to the hard work he put in on a DIY basis — including installing his own underfloor central heating. We find out if it was as difficult as it sounds.

Gordon Wilson has worked hard to achieve the success of his new home in a pretty Midlands town. With its four bedrooms and attached double garage with rooms in the roof, it is close on 230m^2. A solid brick house, where attention to detail rather than complexity of shape is the main attraction, it is now estimated to be worth close to £200,000 – and cost Gordon just over £80,000 to build! No mean accomplishment but one that has required Gordon to muck in and do a fair bit of the work himself, including the underfloor central heating.

The first question has to be — why did you specify underfloor heating in the first place?

Quite simply, I hate radiators. They always seem to be in the wrong place, interfere with furnishing arrangements and provide localised rather than generalised heat. From the moment I first saw the underfloor systems demonstrated, I knew that was what I wanted. Now that I'm actually installing it, I can see why people might opt for radiators upstairs but I've decided to go the whole hog and have it on both floors. The trouble is that upstairs with timber joists, you have to work backwards a bit. On the ground floor it's relatively simple. We've got a beam and block floor that's screeded. We screwed battens to it with silicone under each one to stop creaking. You need a good hammer drill for that as well as the type of plug that enables you to screw right through the batten and push the plugs through into the floor, otherwise it would take forever. The battens are 50mm^2 to match the depth of the insulation. I found that what was sold as 50mm^2 at the merchants was actually undersized, so we bought larger timber and had it planed down – I do not want gaps and creaks in the floor.

The insulation goes in as two layers, each of 25mm. When the first layer is in, you fit the channel clips for the pipe through into the battens. The clips come prenailed in 400mm lengths but I found that when I tried to fit them I couldn't get as close to the batten as I wanted, so I took the original nails out and renailed them tight to the edge.

It's important to follow the plans precisely, otherwise you'll get in a hell of a muddle. Where the pipe loops around at the ends of the zone and crosses the joists, you have to mark the second layer of polystyrene and cut out a channel for the pipe – it's all fairly easy really. For the rest of the lengths, the second layer of insulation just sits tight between the pipes running down each edge of the batten.

Presumably the aluminium sheets on top of that, underneath the chipboard flooring, dissipate and evenly distribute the heat?

That's the idea. As you lay them you have to carefully mark the battens so as not to screw down into the pipe. We screwed all of the chipboard down. I felt that was a better job and, once we'd done that, we marked the boards with the pipe positions as well, especially where they loop across and through the notch in the battens.

Is the pipe difficult to manage? It looks quite heavy.

It is quite cumbersome but they supply a turntable to put each spool on and you pull it off that. The only slight criticism I have is that the coach bolt on the turntable could be a little longer – with the pipe on it, it tends to bind and put all the weight on the casters, making it difficult to turn. I'll change the bolt myself for the top floor. Other than that, it's been a bit of a doddle. I'd warn people to check the manifold valves before they fit them. They're delivered open and the polystyrene packing gets into

"It's important to follow the plans precisely, otherwise you'll get in a hell of a muddle..."

them. If you didn't notice that, it could cause endless problems.

When you fill up the pipe to test it, it is recommended that you do so by connecting a hose to the bleed valve. However, it is a one way valve and kept on popping shut – I had to take the valve out and pull the popper back up before reconnecting.

Talking of manifolds, I've got two, one for each floor zone, each prefitted with actuator valves which alter the flow and therefore the temperature in each room, according to the settings on the individual room thermostats.

What firing system will you use?

A wall mounted gas boiler in the utility room. I thought about a condensing boiler but they're so expensive. I'm going for an unvented system, though – none of that tank in the roof stuff. All in all, I'm very pleased with my choice, David Robbens Ltd. It's been hard work but as long as you follow the plans to the letter and read the instruction manual, there shouldn't be many problems — plus, there's full support from the suppliers. ■

Planning restrictions didn't stop an Essex couple building a contemporary style individual family home — all on a modest budget.

Words:
Debbie Jeffery

Photography:
Nigel Rigden

The house is ▶
situated in a
conservation area
which largely
dictated its
external
appearance.
However, Paul
and Hilary have
created strong
contemporary
interiors to
satisfy their own
tastes.

You may have very strong ideas about the kind of house you prefer to live in — but so have the planners in some situations. This can cause a few headaches for self-builders such as Paul and Hilary Gladman, who were keen to build a contemporary style home in Essex. Their plot is situated in a conservation area bordering National Trust land and the couple recognised that a bold, avant-garde design would be unlikely to gain approval in such a sensitive location.

"We purchased the land in 1998 for £125,000, just before house prices in this area began to soar," explains Hilary. "At that time a dilapidated 1930s bungalow stood on the plot, which most people viewed with the aim of extending and renovating. Paul saw the opportunity to replace it with a new house, however, and took a calculated risk — purchasing the property by sealed bid without any planning consent, and with only a letter from the duty planning officer saying that, in principle, he was happy with the idea." After a long and frustrating planning application, the Gladmans finally won permission exactly one year after first applying — and without having to make any changes to their original plans.

"I designed and drew all the plans myself," says Paul, a builder and house designer by profession, who originally studied civil engineering and had previously built a four bedroom house for himself and Hilary at the tender age of 21. "Having kept the exterior of the house in a traditional chalet style, which reflected the architecture of other properties in the area, I drew inspiration from the American style of living for our interiors — where the kitchen and family room are the focal point of the house, with one space flowing freely into another."

The ground floor follows this principle as closely as the brick and block structure would allow, with the kitchen leading into a two storey glazed oak breakfast room/conservatory and then, in turn, on to the lounge. Double doors open into the hallway, giving the option to close off this area or leave it open plan — visually connected to the lounge by the maple flooring.

Living spaces have been orientated so that windows track the sun through the day, with the breakfast room fully glazed using Pilkington K-glass in order to maximise passive solar gain, whilst bathrooms and service areas are positioned to the north side of the building.

Paul, 38, gave up work to concentrate on building the four bedroom house virtually single-handed, funding the project from savings and using the NHBC's Solo for Self Build warranty.

"I can honestly say that, apart from the plumbing and electrical work, I designed and built every single part of this house myself," he states. "I laid every brick, did all the carpentry work, roof tiling, plastering and fitted all the windows and doors. In fact, I carried out every aspect of the construction. I can stand back with pride and say, 'I built this house.'"

One of the main reasons for moving to Danbury had been the local school, and Paul would deliver his twin sons in the morning before heading off to spend the day on site — even inviting the boys' class for a field trip to see a build in process and (far more important for the average eight year old) try out the Portaloo. "We were lucky enough to be able to stay in our old house during the ▶

FAMILY VALUES

Creating an individual contemporary style home

"Building the house has proved to be an emotionally and physically tiring experience, but worth every moment for the sense of achievement…"

Granite ▲ worktops feature in the kitchen, with decorative wooden spindles custom made by a woodturner for a fraction of the shop price and painted to match the Magnet units.

The oak ▶ framed vaulted breakfast room increases passive solar gain to the open plan layout.

build," says Hilary, who was working as a team administrator at the time, "and this reduced the stresses of self-build enormously for the whole family."

Piled foundations were necessary due to poor ground conditions, including running sand to the front of the house and clay to the rear. Paul had dug boreholes prior to purchasing the land, which revealed the extent and variety of these problems, but he remained undeterred. The external skin of the house is primarily brick. "I prefer solid walls on the ground floor, with a traditional float and set plaster finish," says Paul, who also found the cost of brick and block construction to be less than timber frame in this instance.

Researching materials was an important aspect of the build. Paul feels that too many people base their choices on price alone, and was determined that the bricks and roof tiles should look good together, as well as complementing neighbouring properties and proving acceptable to the planners and conservation officer. Concrete Redland Heathland plain roof tiles have a naturally weathered appearance and imitate clay, allowing him to specify valley and hip tiles and still remain within budget. "It's rather like producing a painting," he explains, "and I tried to echo some of the shades seen in older properties in the area."

The Gladmans had hoped to install oak framed windows but the local authority insisted on white, which they ▶

Useful Contacts

Paul Gladman, designer and builder of contemporary, sustainable houses – Gn^2 (Green's Not Square): 01245 223489

BSG Building Supplies: 01702 544212

Floor joists etc. – Basildon Timber: 01268 591030

Structural calculations – Len Bigg Partnership: 01245 329902

Roof trusses – Flight Timber: 01787 222336

Plasterboard & plastering products – Penlaws: 01268 764029

Sand and aggregates – Tony Bates: 07860 510008

Oak conservatory and internal doors – Advanced Joinery: 01702 542008

PVCu Windows – Goldiva Windows: 02476 695533

K-glass for conservatory – Pilkington Glass: 01268 288551

Sandblasted glass for internal doors – United Glass: 01268 778111

Sanitaryware – Battlesbridge Bathrooms: 01268 573502

Granite worktops and bath surround – Marathon Marble: 01375 841264

Honed slate flooring – Kirkstone: 015394 33296

Limestone for bathroom, glass mosaic tiles – Edgar Udny: 020 8767 8181

White oak staircase – Leigh Stairways: 01702 469066

Kitchen – Magnet: www.magnet.co.uk

Lighting & electrical wholesalers – B. D. C: 01268 727252

Radiators – Bisque: 01225 469244

Timber decking – Brooks Brothers: 01245 226961

Maple flooring – Lambert & Dixson: 01787 379311

Door furniture – Knobs & Knockers: 0151 5234900

Roof tiles – Redland (Heathland Plain tiles): 08705 601000

Bricks – Terca: 0161 873 7701

felt was more in keeping with the surrounding buildings. "We scoured the country and discovered a Coventry-based company who make PVC units to replicate painted softwood, with slim, external Georgian glazing bars," says Hilary, who was keen to avoid the maintenance incurred by painting wooden frames.

The use of natural products was crucial to the interiors, and Paul designed all the internal doors, which are made with sandblasted glass panels, framed by American white oak, allowing light to pass through but also offering privacy. Wardrobes in the master bedroom match these internal doors, with a TV set concealed behind sandblasted glass which has a clear glazed section to enable viewing with the door shut!

Granite, purchased direct from the importer, was chosen for the bath surround and kitchen work surfaces; with honed silver green slate on the kitchen and breakfast room floor and maple flooring covering the rest of the ground floor. The stairs carry on the American white oak theme, with bare wood treads and risers.

"Hilary and I deliberated a great deal over the banisters," says Paul, who enjoyed sourcing the materials. "We didn't want traditional wooden spindles, preferring to use wrought iron in a modern and unconventional way. Eventually we commissioned a simple wave design and had this wire brushed and clear powder coated."

Paul and Hilary are both lovers of contemporary design, and tried to incorporate as much light into the house as possible.

Colour plays an important part internally, with Hilary demonstrating her artistic skills to the full. Although they are twins, the boys each had very different requirements for their bedrooms: Matthew wanted a space theme, and his room has been cleverly designed like the cockpit of a space shuttle, looking out at stars and planets. Ben, on the other hand, has always loved Superman — and this is wonderfully represented in his room using wall murals.

The expensive looking contemporary kitchen was fitted with white Magnet units, around which Hilary and Paul planned the rest of the room — saving over £4,000 by purchasing items from various sources. A central island unit is fitted with a double sink, ceiling beams have been left exposed and painted white, with cable spotlights fitted beneath. "When we first saw these lights we thought they were really innovative," says Hilary, "but now they seem to be everywhere!"

Paul had calculated on market values at the time of purchase that he would expect to make a profit/saving of approximately £100,000, but this figure rose dramatically due to the house price boom in the area. Their house cost a total of £220,000 to build, including land, and has recently been valued at £475,000 — leaving the Gladmans a healthy profit of £255,000, which equates to over 100% investment return.

"You must remember that I virtually built this house single handedly, and made a considerable saving on labour — which is also reflected in the 16 month build time," says Paul. "But, even taking this into account, we are extremely pleased with the outcome and managed to stay within our budget.

"Building the house has proved to be an emotionally and physically tiring experience, but worth every moment for the sense of achievement," he continues. "I wouldn't hesitate to do it again and we have plenty of ideas for future projects. In fact, we are currently hoping to purchase an identical plot only two doors away — and this time we are confident that, not only can we build a sustainable, eco-friendly house, but something which expresses our love of cutting edge contemporary design both inside and out!" ∎

▲ **Wave shaped wrought iron balusters complement the white oak staircase, and were designed by Hilary and Paul, together with the internal doors.**

FLOORPLAN: The kitchen and family room are the focal point of the house, with one space flowing freely into another. The kitchen leads into a two storey glazed oak breakfast room/conservatory, and then in turn on to the lounge. Double doors open into the hallway, giving the option to close off this area or leave it open plan.

First Floor

Ground Floor

Fact File costs as of July 2002

NAMES: Paul and Hilary Gladman

PROFESSIONS: House designer/builder and team administrator

AREA: Essex

HOUSE TYPE: Four bed detached

HOUSE SIZE: 220m^2

BUILD ROUTE: Self

CONSTRUCTION: Brick and block

WARRANTY: NHBC Solo for Self-build

FINANCE: Private

BUILD TIME: 16 months

LAND COST: £125,000

BUILD COST: £81,000

TOTAL COST: £206,000

HOUSE VALUE: £475,000

COST/m^2: £368

57% COST SAVING

A spacious, feature packed home for less than £300/m² — just how did a young Cambridgeshire couple do it?

Words:
Mark Brinkley

Photography:
Jeremy Pembrey

Colin Hussey and Michelle Hayes have built a large and desirable detached house for a price many people would find barely credible. Whereas in many parts of the country, people are straining to achieve build costs under £600/m², Colin and Michelle's self-build project has come in at under half this figure. Unlike many apparently amazingly cheap projects, they didn't spend five years on it — the house was completed in just over a year with 90% of the labour undertaken by subcontractors.

How did they do it? It helps to have good contacts and in this department Colin is blessed. Although he is not and never has been a builder, he is a timber importer and also runs a small builder's merchant so he has access to some amazing deals and many of the materials were purchased at prices that few professional builders would be able to match. He is also on first name terms with many of the local tradesmen in the Peterborough area where he works. In addition, Colin and Michelle managed to buy a plot with foundations already poured at a cost little different to a virgin building plot. In essence, they had around £15,000 of building costs thrown in for next to nothing when they bought the plot.

They found the plot for sale just around the corner from Colin's business. "The guy who was originally going to develop it had a change of heart," says Colin. "He'd bought the plot, a subdivision of an existing garden, got planning permission and poured the foundations back in 1997. But then they did nothing with it for three years and ▶

The plot ▶ already came with foundations poured. Colin and Michelle liked the existing design and saved themselves £15,000.

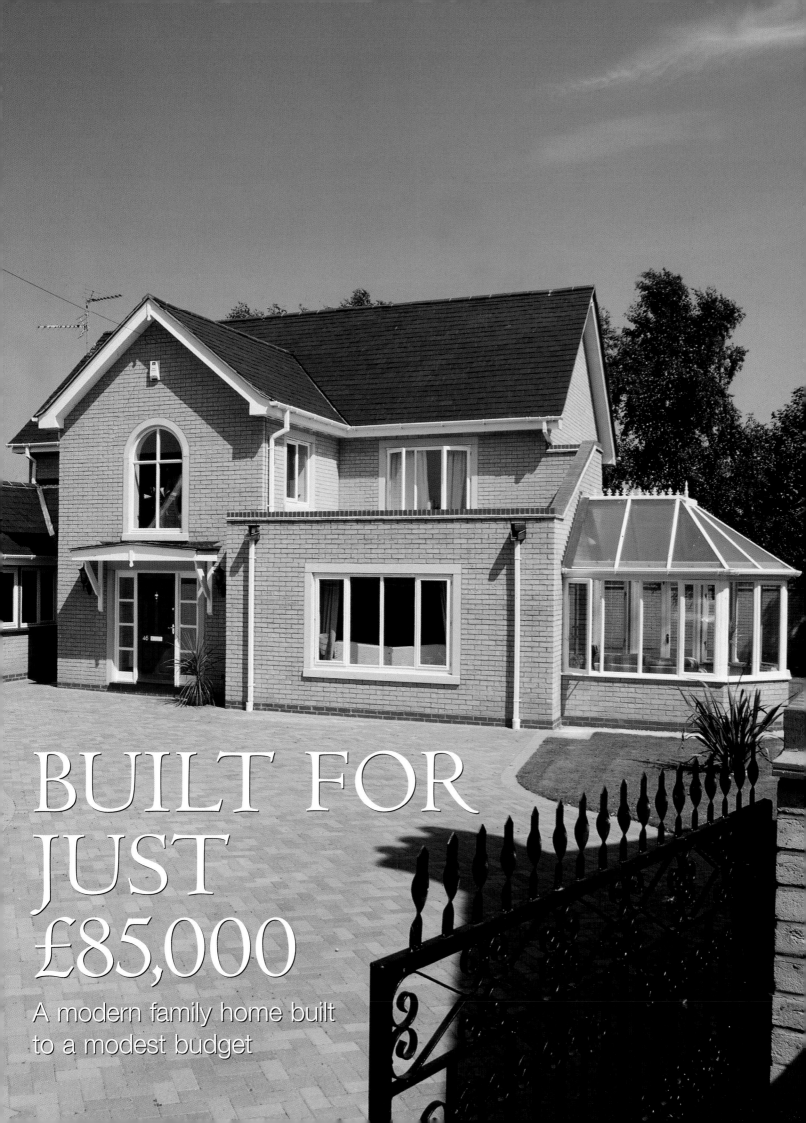

BUILT FOR JUST £85,000

A modern family home built
to a modest budget

"Although we didn't really have any input on the external appearance, internally we controlled a lot."

▲ **The spacious galleried entrance hall (ALSO RIGHT) provides an impressive feature that belies the remarkably low build cost.**

eventually his wife decided she didn't want to live there so they put it on the market early in 2000. By then it had got very overgrown and it didn't look terribly attractive."

"Actually we had no idea just how big this house was when we bought the plot," says Michelle. "It wasn't until we had cleared away all the undergrowth that it finally sunk in just how large it is." After spending the duration of the build, just over a year, camping out in just one room, both of them are still amazed at their good fortune.

They knew when they purchased the plot that they had to build more or less what had already been drawn but that was never a problem because they liked designer Peter Hand's original plans. Nevertheless, their home is situated on the village green and is in a Conservation Area, so the planners took a keen interest in the materials they chose to build the house. Colin managed to source a very attractive Dutch brick, dressed with stone cills from Hanson and topped with a natural slate roof without compromising their tight budget.

In the hall, ▶ Colin and Michelle have built a feature brick wall using old bricks bought from a friend who was demolishing an old house.

"I think our home fits in very well with all the neighbours, even though the style is quite modern," he says. "Although we didn't really have any input on the external appearance, internally we controlled a lot. The house is also a very different design to what is available on the open market. We've got much larger rooms and the kitchens and bathrooms are fitted to a higher standard than you would expect in a developer's house."

One of the most striking features is the use of wooden floors throughout the property. Here, Colin used his knowledge and trade contacts to the full. "We have gone for redwood tongue and grooved boarding. The quality of softwood boarding is extremely variable which is one of the reasons people keep specifying hardwood floors. But if you know what to buy, you can get some really good deals for around half the price of oak or beech."

In the kitchen and the hallway, they have used 200mm wide planks which can be hard to get hold of in the UK. "To get the best softwood floors, you need to buy from the sawmills way up in the north of Sweden or Finland where the timber grows much more slowly and the growth rings are consequently much tighter. That way you get a much harder timber and one much less prone to cupping or warping. But you have to know what you are after and you have to be prepared to wait – it can take up to eight weeks to get hold of the right stuff and get it shipped over here. It bears no comparison to what gets sold as tongue and grooved flooring over here."

The house is built of brick and block construction. Colin is a fan not only of traditional blockwork, but of hard plastered walls as well. "I notice that all my subbies knock the walls when they go into a new house, looking for that tell-tale ring you get from plaster. For them, hard plastered walls are a mark of quality and I respect that."

Almost all the build was carried out by local tradesmen, many of whom knew each other. Michelle and Colin undertook certain parts of the process themselves, such as clearing the site and arranging the materials. In fact getting bricks and blocks onto site proved a significant headache as Colin decided he could do it with the forklift from his ▶

DIY Groundworks

The wettest year on record couldn't have come at a worst time for novice self-builders Dave and Jan Andrews. They're made of stern stuff, though, and are planning to do almost all of the work themselves starting with the groundworks. We let them get it off their chest — and share a few tips.

If ever the indomitable spirit of the self-builder needed applauding then Dave and Jan Andrews would surely be amongst the first in line for the title 'Heroes'. Despite terrible weather, they've struggled on, working weekends and leave times, determined to do their own groundworks.

Dave's in the RAF and, having made little money on their previous homes, he and Jan felt that they needed to build up their equity and the best way to do that was to self-build. They bought the plot in Lincolnshire for £44,500 and are planning to build a 295m² house and garage with a budget of just £90,000 by doing much of the work themselves, hiring in labour only when they absolutely need to.

> "We could only do things at weekends and leave times — and it seemed as if it rained on every one of those days..."

You couldn't have picked a worse year for this, could you?

I'm sick to death of pumping out. This is the worst year on record for rainfall and we've well and truly had our share. Only now, when we're finally getting out of the ground, can we really look forward to some progress. We had to reduce the levels, which meant sending 280 tons of spoil away before we really started. We'd planned to get the footings dug within two weeks but then it started raining for what seemed like forever.

I bought a pump for £99, plus VAT, and that's been a saviour. I also bought a JCB for £1,800. It came with a 300mm and 600mm bucket and a 1,200mm blade. I thought about a 360° machine but they were all too expensive.

What sort of soil conditions have you got and why did you opt for deep strip rather than trenchfill?

It's a heavy, blue-grey clay and because of the trees on the adjoining properties we had to go down to 2.1m in several places. The plans showed a deep strip foundation but when we first started to have the problems I did consider changing to trenchfill. Then events overtook me. The sides of the trenches fell in so often that in the end they were so wide it wouldn't have made financial sense to try to fill them with concrete at £47/m³.

Even when we finally put the concrete in there was so much wet that it flowed around any shuttering I put there. I had to hand dig the final slots for the concrete in the ruins of my trenches and then when we were finally ready to pour in July, it rained again. The clay puddled in the bottom of the trenches and when it eventually stopped and dried out, it cracked and crazed. The Building Inspector wanted all of that dug out, yet again by hand. Even though we were getting on for 2m deep, it's not as dangerous as it sounds because by then the sides of the trench were so wide they resembled a funnel.

We could only do work at weekends and leave times and it seemed as if it rained on every one of those. It wasn't supposed to be like this. We'd built an extension before and I knew what I was letting myself in for but nothing had prepared us for this. When we finally managed to concrete the foundations I had to do it in two bits and even then leave the garage off so that we had a way through to the other footings. We put three starter bars in each end for the garage foundations to be added later and left a rough slump end for a key.

Did you do your own blockwork?

Yes. No problem there, although I'd forgotten just how heavy concrete blocks were. Jan and our sons helped with the labouring but I had to do most of the loading out. Of course, it carried on raining and the trenches kept on filling up. We'd had to dig a hole for a soil test before we started and we connected that to the trenches and used it as a sump so that we could pump out from that into the road drains. I did find though that as the trenches were by now so wide it was difficult to judge the levels and I went wrong in a few places. We had to slice quite a few of the blocks to get to the proper dpc level.

Any regrets or tips for others?

Plenty. With hindsight we should have gone straight to trenchfill and filled it right away rather than waiting. But I just didn't expect monsoon conditions and the damage that they can cause in just a week. The JCB has paid for itself. I cleared the site of 450mm of hardcore before we even started to dig and that would have cost a fortune if I'd have had to pay someone else to do it. I'm not doing the brickwork or the roof. I'll labour on others for those trades but we'll be doing our own electrics and plumbing and the 2nd fix. ■

Words: **Debbie Jeffery**   Photography: **Nigel Rigden**

A Five Bedroom Home for £97,000!

A fantastic value timber frame home

A well-scheduled project meant that Nevelle and Debbie Marchent's spacious family home was completed on budget and in just seven months.

Determination drove Nevelle and Debbie Marchent to keep on searching for that elusive plot in their home county of Somerset. "Like many couples we had dreamed of building our own house," says Nevelle. He and Debbie are keen DIY enthusiasts who had already modified, decorated and extended previous homes, and self-build seemed the next logical step.

"We found a plot initially but couldn't sell our own in time, so we had to pull out, and a long search began," says Debbie. "During all this time we made plans and prepared budgets, as well as researching timber frame kit suppliers," says Nevelle, managing director of the Crypton Technology Group. "We had decided on a timber frame system, as it seemed to simplify the daunting task of building a house, and eventually settled on Potton to supply our kit."

Impressed with the Potton homes they had seen in magazines, Debbie and Nevelle visited the company's show site — asking them to draw up plans to suit a variety of prospective plots. The couple took a standard house design and then proceeded to substantially modify this — increasing the overall size by enlarging the inner hallway ▶

▲ A timber frame was chosen for the quick build time and high insulation levels, with support from Potton giving the Marchents added confidence.

69

A Five Bedroom Home for £97,000

"We spent time specifying each job, down to the position of electrical sockets, to prevent any budget overruns…"

▲ **The Marchents wanted lots of circulation space and so they decided to modify the standard Potton floorplan accordingly.**

and landing areas. Whilst many modern homes try to minimise such circulation spaces, the Marchents felt these areas to be an important part of daily life.

Final external details would be dictated by planning conditions and the site, but the outline plans were now in place. All the Marchents needed was a plot! After nine months, and several abortive attempts to buy land, Debbie spotted a small classified advert for two building plots only a mile from their rented accommodation.

"We jumped into the car straight away and took a quick look before contacting the agent," Debbie explains. "The pair of plots were a quarter of an acre in size, with main road frontage, mains drainage nearby and planning permission for two semi-detached houses." The level site is screened by mature trees and bordered by greenfield land, with a stream running along the rear boundary. It was clear that this was exactly what they were looking for.

"After checking that we would be able to get planning permission for a single five bedroom dwelling we put in an

offer for the double plot, with planning as a condition of purchase," says Nevelle. Following various delays the sale was finally completed in May 1999, and permission granted for a dormer roofed version of Potton's Waterford design — with a fifth bedroom above the integral garage.

After several years of waiting, the Marchents could finally start to build. "Our preparation work meant that we had already identified and secured local contractors," says Nevelle, who intended to procure materials, manage the trades and carry out all 'fill-in' tasks himself. "We spent a considerable amount of time specifying each job, right down to the position of electrical sockets, to prevent any budget overruns."

On May 7th the family spent the entire day making an entrance hole in the hedge by hand for the ground-workers, who then proceeded to clear the entire site with their machines within an hour the following day! Ground-work and foundations preparation was tackled in mostly good weather, although it then poured with rain for the whole weekend that Nevelle spent tidying up the footings, ensuring that he was repeatedly soaked.

The frame was delivered on June 7th. "We elected to use Potton's own erection team, who lived locally, which

The spacious kitchen/breakfast room is often the centre of activity, and will be extended with a conservatory in the future.

saved on accommodation costs," says Debbie. "This proved to be one of the most exciting parts of the build, with the house changing shape each day. Unfortunately we also experienced our first break-in to the site hut, when some tools and Velux windows were stolen. Luckily Potton quickly arranged replacements so work was not held up."

Nevelle spent two weeks on the site in order to quickly resolve any queries and maintain contact with Potton, so that any problems would not escalate or delay the build. "Final planning changes had introduced a dormer roof detail, and some of the first floor panels had not been produced to the later, modified version," says Nevelle. "The problem was rapidly identified, however, and the local team carried out on-site modifications, guided by Potton's site managers."

At this stage Nevelle began priming and staining the external timbers. The plumber and electrician were able to commence first fix immediately upon the frame's completion, whilst the roof was felted and tiled. "This was when we discovered just how many noggins there are in a timber frame house," laughs Nevelle, who was responsible for this not inconsiderable task. He also tackled the dry-lining – having previously attended the dry-lining course

run by plasterboard manufacturer, Lafarge – so insulation, vapour barrier and plasterboard work began inside whilst the bricklayers erected the external brick and block walls.

"It was during this time that we really appreciated the role of the Zurich inspector," says Debbie. "He provided advice on building standards and assisted us throughout, sanctioning the mortgage stage payments." As the house was being built on a tight budget it was vital for the Marchents to regularly monitor progress to ensure that they remained on course.

The work rate became quite hectic, with daily trips to the builders' merchants and hours spent co-ordinating trades and deliveries. "I was working long hours during the week, which meant that late evenings and weekends became routine," says Nevelle, who would often start at 5.30am. "It was exhausting, but the adrenaline moves you on, and the sense of achievement is terrific. We were a good team, with Debbie making soft furnishings and curtains for every room in the house, working as a school secretary and looking after the boys."

By mid-August the house was ready for external rendering and internal skim plaster to ceilings and walls, with the plasterer working in rotation with other trades ▶

throughout September. The second fix carpentry and plumbing started, and the installation of the staircase felt like a real occasion. Finally the Marchents could show their friends around without asking them to use a ladder!

Once Nevelle had fitted the rainwater goods it was time to dismantle the scaffolding. The sealed system Worcester Bosch combination gas boiler was installed, and has proved an excellent choice — with low running costs and instant hot water at all times. Nevelle fitted the kitchen at the end of October, enlisting the carpenter's help with the worktops. "I spent the following month painting and coving each room, and completing various other jobs as our moving in date loomed," he recalls.

With the painting completed and the carpets fitted, the family finally moved into their house on December 7th — just seven months after building work had begun. "After all our hard work," says Debbie, "we can finally sit back and enjoy our new house. The pride we feel in achieving our goal is terrific, and we would definitely consider self-building again — it has all been so worthwhile." ■

Fact File costs as of December 2002

NAMES: Nevelle and Deborah Marchent

PROFESSIONS: Company director and school secretary

AREA: Somerset

HOUSE TYPE: 5 bedroom detached

HOUSE SIZE: 237m² + garage

BUILD ROUTE: Self-managed subcontractors and DIY

CONSTRUCTION: Timber frame

WARRANTY: Zurich

FINANCE: Norwich & Peterborough BS

BUILD TIME: May – December 1999

LAND COST: £65,000

BUILD COST: £97,000

TOTAL COST: £162,000

HOUSE VALUE: £330,000

51% COST SAVING

COST/m²: £409

Cost Breakdown:

Foundations & aggregate	£8,133
Timber frame kit	£35,500
External build	£14,392
Roof	£4,000
Internal finishing/drylining	£6,084
Plumbing/heating	£4,520
Electrical & fittings	£2,871
Kitchen	£4,600
Sanitaryware	£2,000
Driveway & fencing/gates	£4,000
Tiles	£2,000
Fitted wardrobes	£4,000
Scaffold	£1,200
Services	£700
Miscellaneous	£3,000
TOTAL	**£97,000**

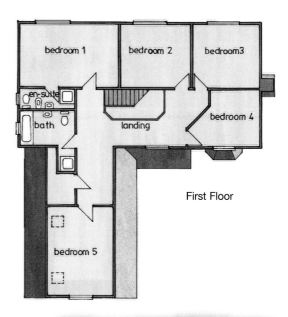

First Floor

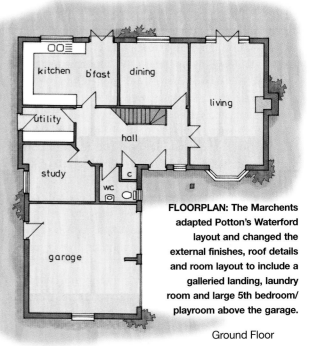

FLOORPLAN: The Marchents adapted Potton's Waterford layout and changed the external finishes, roof details and room layout to include a galleried landing, laundry room and large 5th bedroom/playroom above the garage.

Ground Floor

USEFUL CONTACTS: **Timber frame kit** - Potton Ltd: 01480 401401; **Building supplies** - Jewson: 0800 539766; - Travis Perkins: 0161 7368751; **Sanitaryware** - City Plumbing: 01823 282565; **Garage doors etc.** - Screwfix: 0500 414141; **Paint** - Dulux: 01753 550555; **Drylining (training course)** - Lafarge: 01275 377789; **Kitchen** - MFI: 0870 6075093; **Fitted bedroom furniture** - Wickes: 0870 6089001; **Electrical items** - City Electrical Factors: 01823 259177; **Fireplace surround** - Plasterworks: 01823 326694

DIY Carpentry

Surrey self-builders Clive and Noi Harris saved a fortune on their bungalow after taking on many of the trades themselves. We asked them to share their experience of undertaking the second fix carpentry.

After three years, Clive and Noi Harris can sit back, say that they have finally finished their self-build in Surrey and look forward to the next — only this one will be in Australia, to where they're shortly emigrating. For their UK project they laid most of the blocks themselves, with Noi doing all of the weatherstruck pointing. They helped their carpenter with the roof, did all of the first and second fix carpentry, tiled, tacked and carried out the plumbing and electrics in their entirety. And their reward? A lovely home that's just sold for £325,000 at a cost of just £165,000 — a huge equity gain. We spoke to them about the carpentry work.

Presumably as you've done so much work you had previous experience?

Only the usual DIY and we only used normal DIY tools, other than a semi professional circular saw which I am glad I bought. Our first real involvement was fitting the windows – we chose triple glazed windows from Swedhus because of the road noise. It was simple really, just drilling and plugging. The thing is, they don't have cills and they're not grooved for a window board. Inside, I had to drill and dowel the boards, then strap them down with brackets, which were later plastered in. Outside, I bought the hardwood cill sections, routed out to fit the brickwork, drilled again and doweled them to the windows with a mastic seal. Lining up the dowels was tricky until I fitted metal plugs to the pins and pressed the board home to mark the point for drilling.

With the windows fitted you were weathertight and could get on inside.

Yes. The first thing we did was to put in the chipboard loft flooring and the studwork. Technically it's just storage up there and we can't have windows or rooflights but we've divided it into rooms nonetheless. I nailed the boards down but now wish that I'd screwed them down as we do have creaks. After that it was back outside again to finish the porch, which is in green oak from a chap in the village. It was supposed to have the lintel in oak but the warranty inspector was really hot on all timber being stamped and certified, so we had to lower the beam and put a graded softwood lintel above it. The internal doors were reclaimed Victorian panelled that we had stripped. I had to cut them down before we could even start to hang them. In the end the latches are quite close to the dowel joints but they're pretty substantial things. I tried to cut out for the latches and butts with a router but reverted in the end to hammer and chisel.

And you presumably fitted all your own skirting and architrave?

The problem there was the warping of the timber both ways. I tried to glue the skirting at first but it just pulled away, so I drilled, plugged and screwed in the end. At first, I mitred the inside corners but then I realised that it was better to scribe them. It's a bit fiddly with moulded timber but it makes a better job. I did mitre mid wall joints though. With the architrave, I again glued it but I made the mistake of gluing it to the plasterwork as well as the lining. I realise now that the architrave is meant to mask the joint between the lining and the plaster and that by doing so I transposed the movement to beyond the architrave.

Presumably you put the oak flooring down before you did the skirting?

No, I'd discounted using oak flooring at first as it was too expensive but then we got the VAT back and went to a show where they had a special offer. I actually missed out on the VAT reclaim for it anyway! It's laid on a compressible vapour barrier and is quite simple in that the planks clip to each other and are glued at the

> "The carpenter wanted to cut the landing trimmer. 'Not on your Nelly', I thought..."

butt ends. They supply a special tool for the cramping but we still found we had to improvise to get it really tight. The thing is, you have to leave a 15mm gap at the edge that's normally masked by the skirting. As that was already in, I had to get some oak moulding and put that all around the edge. At the same time I got some 50x25mm oak and carved out my own thresholds with a router. In fact, that proved handy because when it came to fit the kitchen units, the worktop edges got damaged so I used the same moulding to make edging strips.

Fitting the kitchen was relatively easy. It worked well, even if I did have some trouble lining the units up with the hatch opening. I didn't do the staircase but I did get involved. There wasn't enough headroom and the carpenter wanted to cut the landing trimmer. 'Not on your Nelly', I thought, even though he assured me he was experienced in these things. In the end, I did it myself at the other end by trimming out one more ceiling joist. ∎

Being willing to shop around for materials and get involved in every aspect of their self-build has saved Jacolyn and Ash Tankaria a fortune.

Words:
Debbie Jeffery

Photography:
Paul Dixon

▲ The Tankarias demolished an ugly extended cottage on a village plot, which has been replaced with an attractive cottage-style property on three floors.

Building houses has become something of a way of life for Jacolyn and Ash Tankaria, who are currently working on their third project with a fourth already planned. "I can honestly say that we have enjoyed every minute spent on site," Jacolyn states. "I wake up in the morning and can't wait to get started. Tackling every aspect of a self-build is physically and mentally challenging, but we find the whole process very exciting."

After being made redundant Ash went on a course to learn bricklaying for six months – something he had always wanted to do. He excelled at the bricklaying course and was presented with a silver trowel to mark his achievements. Ash and Jacolyn had renovated numerous old properties in the past but now, with his newly acquired skills, Ash was keen to build a house from scratch. The result was an impressive six bedroom Georgian style property in Newbury which the couple designed and built in its entirety.

Jacolyn Tankaria had worked for a chartered surveyor some years before, and had picked up some useful tips along the way. She decided to draw up the plans and produce the building regulations drawings herself. "Once I started I found that I was actually quite good at it," she smiles. "I did approach an architect for advice on the trickier aspects of the design, such as the staircase, but I was soon able to work alone." ▶

"Built for £38,000!"

Achieving great value on a DIY self-build

"The kitchen tiles we brought over from France, where we shop about once a month. You can achieve the same look as more expensive interiors for a fraction of the price..."

"We both needed to work full time, as well as tackling every aspect of the build ourselves. It took almost five years for us to complete." Ash explains. "We loved that house but, unfortunately, new neighbours arrived who were impossible to live with, so we decided to move on and build again."

The couple purchased a rundown property with three acres of land in Kent, with the intention of 'bungalow eating' and building a replacement dwelling. Once again Jacolyn drew up the plans for the new house, but this time luck was not on their side. The bungalow is situated in an Area of Outstanding Natural Beauty, necessitating strict

planning procedures. "We were living in the damp, grotty bungalow and, although we had permission to replace it with a similar building, we soon realised that gaining planning consent for anything else was going to take some time," admits Ash.

Rose Cottage, in the tiny village of West Hougham, just over a mile from the Tankarias' bungalow, seemed to offer the ideal solution: temporary accommodation while the couple went to appeal to gain approval for the house they wanted to build. "We first viewed Rose Cottage in the summer and planned to renovate it and live there for a short time," Jacolyn explains. "Unfortunately the cottage turned out to be almost as damp and rundown as the bungalow! We were stuck between a rock and a hard place."

Bravely, she and Ash decided to knock down the property and build a five bedroom cottage-style replacement as a stop gap. Gaining planning permission for this venture proved quick and easy, with Jacolyn using design details from their previous project. She rotated the footprint so that it sat across the compact site and added a second floor in the attic, lit by Velux windows, which accommodates a large multi-purpose playroom. "I spent about 15 hours drawing up the plans — starting in the morning and working until midnight," she explains. "I find that if you keep things simple and don't specify too much it seems to be more successful."

Planning and building regulation approval were granted within six weeks, and the Tankarias soon set to work. Once again they decided to handle all of the building work themselves. "The only thing we didn't do was to connect up the gas boiler," says Ash. "Other than that we

Cost Breakdown

Footings	£2,091	
Bricks	£4,822	
NHBC	£1,191	
Moving electricity supply	£352	
Oversite concrete	£1,307	
Blocks	£3,502	
Wall ties	£100	
Wall insulation	£394	
Jablite	£374	
Lintels	£481	
Staircase parts	£464	
Flue liner	£226	
Sand and ballast	£594	
Cement	£377	
DPC	£93	
Windows and external doors	£3,922	
First fix timber and fixings	£535	
Roof timber and fixings	£3,502	
Roof tiles and lead	£3,331	
Guttering	£440	
Drains	£580	
Heat cables	£75	
Central Heating and water	£1,931	
Kitchen	£701	
Sanitaryware	£862	
Internal doors and 2nd fix timber	£1,737	
Electrics	£580	
Plasterboard, plaster and adhesives	£1,655	
Roof insulation	£218	
Chipboard flooring	£615	
Paint and wall tiles	£601	
Gas supply	£302	
Miscellaneous	£209	
TOTAL	**£38,164**	

tackled everything from demolition to decorating, closely following the NHBC Solo handbook."

The National House Building Council's Solo for Self Build warranty and insurance policy has been designed to protect the self-builder during the building process and provide cover for ten years after completion. Solo offers the freedom to arrange for the building work to be done by individual contractors or to undertake some or all of the work yourself, which was exactly what the Tankarias needed.

Jacolyn is a determined lady. In addition to working as a market research interviewer and looking after five children she undertook the setting out, laboured daily on site alongside Ash and purchased all the materials. "A strict budget was vital and it was important to shop around for the best possible deals on materials," she says. "It could be frustrating and involved a great deal of phoning, but the savings were enormous. One builder's merchant gave me a 45% discount on our windows, and the overburnt yellow bricks we chose were far cheaper than 'perfect' bricks and give a more aged appearance. I had an account with Travis Perkins to secure trade prices but paid using my credit card, which gives back 1%. It all soon adds up."

Demolishing the existing cottage was a new experience for the couple, who sold everything from the old floorboards to Kent peg tiles through the local free paper. "The whole building was perilously close to collapse, and we were so glad that we had decided against renovating — it was unbelievable that it had stayed up for so long!" says Ash. "Everything was sold apart from the 'Rose Cottage' name sign and a fireplace, which we adapted and used in the new house."

Clay soil necessitated deep foundations, but the biggest problem proved to be the weather: it poured with rain on the day the Tankarias began digging the footings and the

"I estimated a total of £47,000 and we actually spent £9,000 less."

deluge continued unabated for the next few weeks. "Laying the bricks and blocks proved relatively easy, but we needed help when it came to the roof trusses," says Ash. "Luckily a neighbour was able to advise us, although a howling gale was blowing on the day the crane was due to lift the attic trusses into position. It was January, and we had to brush the snow from the rafters before we could put the felt and battens on!'

It was Jacolyn who tiled the roof with French plain clay tiles. "I had worked on the roof of our previous house using slates, but this proved slightly different," she explains. "It was a learning curve, and working high up in ▶

▲ The kitchen was built using components from various suppliers in order to keep costs down.

▲ Overburnt bricks and plain clay roof tiles ensure that the new house fits well into its surroundings.

anything. Bathroom suites are B&Q's cheapest value packs which we dressed up with mixer taps. The kitchen tiles we brought over from France, where we shop about once a month. You can achieve the same look as more expensive interiors for a fraction of the price if you are prepared to shop around."

Incredibly, the final build cost for the 229m² Rose Cottage was just £38,000, with many of the materials costing even less than Jackie had initially budgeted. "I estimated a total of £47,000 and we actually spent £9,000 less," she remarks. There is a first for everything.

"Once we had finished building the cottage we moved in for a year and have just sold it for £310,000 to the first person who viewed it, giving us an overall profit of over £200,000. We have finally obtained planning permission for our other site and are currently in the process of building a lambing shed on the land, which will eventually be used for holiday lets, before we tackle the main house. Self-building has literally changed our lives and transformed our bank balance — why would we want to stop now?" ∎

the winter was not pleasant. We attended exhibitions and read lots of DIY books for advice as we went along — although these frequently contradicted each other!"

Once the shell of the house was complete Ash and Jacolyn turned their attention to fitting out the interiors. "We spent a lot of money on tools and Ash is a complete perfectionist," says Jacolyn. "When it came to fitting the kitchen we pieced it together using cheap MFI carcasses, drawer packs from Screwfix and Magnet's oak doors which we had purchased in a sale. We didn't splash out on

FLOORPLAN: The cottage-style property benefits from five bedrooms, with the roofspace (not shown) offering a flexible space in the form of a large playroom which can be used for TV, music, computers and additional guest accommodation.

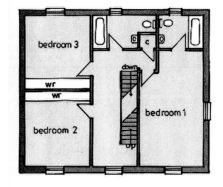

First Floor

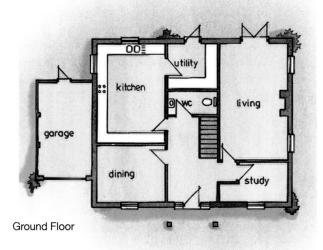

Ground Floor

Fact File costs as of March 2003

NAMES:	Jacolyn and Ash Tankaria
PROFESSIONS:	Market research interviewer
AREA:	Kent
HOUSE TYPE:	Five bedroom detached
HOUSE SIZE:	229m²
BUILD ROUTE:	Selves
CONSTRUCTION:	Brick and block

WARRANTY:	NHB
SAP RATING:	97
FINANCE:	Private
BUILD TIME:	19 months
LAND COST:	£71,209
BUILD COST:	£38,169
TOTAL COST:	£109,378
HOUSE VALUE:	£310,000
COST/m²:	£167

65% COST SAVING

USEFUL CONTACTS: **Bricks and roof tiles** – Coastal Brick: 01304 827722; **Roof trusses** – Dover Trusses: 01303 844303; **Various materials** – Screwfix: 0500 414141; **Windows** – Travis Perkins: 01303 271122; Jewsons: 01304 204444; **Roof windows** – The Velux Co. Ltd.: 01592 772211; **Insulation** – Rockwool Ltd: 01656 862621; **Kitchen** – Magnet: 01535 661133; **Warranty** – National House Building Council (NHBC): 01494 434477

DIY Flooring

Dave and Joy Stanley did much of their own work on their Midlands self-build. Laying their own timber floor was one of the trickier jobs — but it saved them both time and money.

Dave and Joy Stanley have long since given up the idea of 'normal' weekends in favour of continuing work on their new four bedroom house overlooking the Severn valley in the Midlands. However, we were interested in Dave's experience of laying solid oak floorboards made from reclaimed timber.

All the DIY jobs the Stanleys have done has meant they could build a house worth £200,000 on a lovely spot in the middle of open countryside for just £125,000, including land. In itself, the laying of this flooring hasn't really saved that much cash — about four working days (£3-400) is the consensus — but it is a job that even the most reluctant DIY self-builder could take on — providing they follow Dave's advice and avoid the common pitfalls that await.

Yes, but there was a long search for the right sort of flooring. We'd come from an old cottage that we loved and, whilst we knew that we wanted a modern house, we still wanted to retain the sort of character we had before. So much of the wooden flooring that we saw was too modern and clinical – varnished laminate and the like – and would never have suited us. Not only that but we have a small, growing daughter plus two large and boisterous dogs – much of what we looked at just wouldn't have stood up to the punishment they can dish out.

It wasn't until we discovered a firm called Mick Jones Timber did we realise that a solid oak floor was what we had been looking for. Mick Jones specialise in tongued and grooved planks of seasoned oak cut from old reclaimed beams. Finished simply with wax, their flooring looks old and, whilst a slight scratch on a varnished floor could ruin it, even a deep groove only adds to these boards' character. All the dogs can do is improve it!

Had you ever laid anything like this before?

No, I was conscious of the fact that with this there was never going to be any cover up. I'd helped with the kitchen tiles but there the principle is quite different, in that you square off the room and work out from the centre. Here, because of the necessary expansion gap all around the outside and the fact that you have to fit the boards together, that wasn't possible.

The only choice was to block out from one wall and then work from that. The problem is, there's no guarantee that all the rooms are square, so I had to carefully measure it all out and in a couple of places start with a cut board to even out the discrepancy. With long boards 170mm wide, if I hadn't done that, particularly in the hall, it would have showed up alarmingly. As it was, the only place where it does is just by the fireplace but there it doesn't really matter as we are having a hearthrug.

So having worked it all out, how did the actual laying process go? Was it difficult?

It was very heavy work. The planks are 4-5m long in random lengths and 170mm wide by 22mm thick. Oak, especially old oak like this, is very heavy. Although it was fairly uniform, it was dished and in places some of the planks were curved along the length. I had laid the first five rows in the lounge before I discovered that I'd been laying them upside down. There's a bevelled edge to one side of the tongue and I realised then that it's there to help you to ease the board down at an angle and into the groove.

I've got a really good cross cut saw which was a boon and, although the boards aren't laid to joists, I thought it was important to line up the joins and the fixings so was trying to get things

"I had laid the first five rows before I discovered that I'd been laying them upside down..."

square in both directions. I think I've succeeded quite well. I would fit the board in at one end then drill and fix it in situ as I knelt on it, before manoeuvring myself along the board, pushing the tongue home as I went. With some of them I really had to force them in by levering on a chisel but most of them just tapped home. I screwed each one then plugged them using plugs made with an attachment I've got with my drill.

In some ways, the fact that I was screwing down to chipboard made things easier. I laid double sided rubber tape on the deck at 250mm intervals. With the gap at the edge hidden by the skirtings, which have happily stained to the same colour, it really looks a treat.

Did you have to stain it?

No, we just waxed it and it's given a perfect finish. We're thrilled with it. Well, most of us are – our daughter, Phoebe, came home from where she'd been staying during the weekend we did it. I asked her what she thought of it. "Yes Daddy, that's nice," she said. "It'll look even nicer when the carpet's down." ■

"Did you always plan to have a timber ground floor, with the exception of the tiled kitchen and utility room?"

Building with reclaimed materials

THE NEW OLD

Anne and Robert Waterfall have built a traditional style farmhouse that already looks at least a century old thanks to the use of reclaimed materials.

Farmers Anne and Robert Waterfall knew it would be difficult to leave the rambling old farmhouse they had lived in for 25 years when the time came to retire and hand the reins to their nephew. So 20 years ago the couple invested in a plot of land on a hillside just four miles from the farm so that, one day, they could build their dream home overlooking the countryside they loved so much.

When the time finally came to move, they invited an architect to draw up plans for a Victorian style farmhouse which would look as though it had been there for generations, and give them a flavour of the home they were reluctantly leaving behind.

The result is a hilltop house built entirely of reclaimed bricks, stone and ready-mossed roof tiles, complete with windows which look as though they have replaced original barn doors, intricately detailed gable ends and Victorian air bricks. Anyone given directions to the "newly-built house on the hill" could be forgiven for driving straight past it thinking it had been there for more than a century.

Even those who step inside may be fooled by the 16-foot high vaulted ceiling and Queen post trusses in the airy kitchen, the lower-than-average architraves and the latched wooden doors.

"We wanted to recreate the character of a Victorian farmhouse without the five bedrooms we had before – far too much to clean – and the inevitable draughts," says Anne. "We particularly wanted a large kitchen. Traditionally, all the farm business is carried out around the kitchen table and we wanted to keep that as the focal point of the family home."

The Waterfalls were granted planning permission to build the house on the basis of an agricultural tie, a condition ▶

Words:
Heather Dixon
Photography:
Jeremy Phillips

HOUSE

"Building was a great experience and nowhere near as traumatic as people said it would be…"

Green oak ▲ beams help to give the new house traditional character.

that only a working or retired farmer, or the farmer's wife, could live in it. This suited the couple, who were maintaining a working interest in the farm.

"We decided to manage the project ourselves," says Robert. "I had been managing a farm all my life and the principles were the same – you just have to be organised. It is a case of managing men, money and materials. The architect understood exactly what we wanted – he was renowned for designing houses with character – and from the basis of his initial drawings the house simply evolved.

"There were no detailed plans to work from. We simply made decisions as we went along, subcontracting the work and managing it all from the outset. I did as much work as I could myself to keep costs to a minimum and Anne knew instinctively what looked right, so we worked as a team. We were never daunted by the prospect. If you want to do something enough, you get on and do it."

Imported two- ▶ inch French bricks, which cost 60p each, were sandblasted before being used to create the impressive chimney breast over the Aga.

The Waterfalls spent many weekends scouring reclamation yards for materials, taking the architect's advice of thinking "chunky, chunky" so that everything was in proportion to the property's dimensions to give it a solid feel.

One of their best finds was a batch of 16,000 handmade bricks from a redundant Victorian threshing barn. "We went to see the barn before it was down to see what the bricks looked like en masse," says Robert. "We also counted them to make sure there were enough for our needs."

Another demolition site was removing stone cills and mullions from a former gentleman's residence, which were perfect for the Waterfalls' dream house. Through word of mouth the couple gradually managed to source other materials which would add to the authentic feel of their home, including stone, roof tiles and 75 matching ridge tiles designed to the Victorians' favourite 50° angle.

They dug most of the foundations themselves, hiring a digger and using farm vehicles to take away the spoil. Shortly after the footings were laid, the rains came down and the site turned into a quagmire. "Every morning we had to pump out the water so the bricklayers could lay the foundation blocks," says Robert.

It took the bricklayers six months to complete the walls, but their attention to detail was extraordinary. They used lime and yellow sand in the mortar to give it an aged look and created decorative courses and corbelling to add character. The roof is finished in different heights so all the timbers were specially cut and made on site before the roof was assembled at a 'barn raising' celebration. ▶

The staircase ▶
was built by a
local joinery firm
and assembled
on site in
sections. The
spindles were
chosen for their
chunky design
which suited the
style of the
house.

The build hit a delay of several weeks while the windows were being made and Robert was harvesting, but the Waterfalls were in no hurry. By the time the project started to move again, the pace quickened considerably and the house soon took shape inside.

Robert and Anne were keen to include a range of green oak timbers which they sourced in Shropshire and designed themselves to create beautiful open trusses and tenant joists in the kitchen and beams in many of the rooms. They treated and sanded all except the hall beam before they were installed.

"Unfortunately, we learned the hard way with the hall beam and ended up sanding it once it was in. Have you ever tried to use a heavy sander over your head while balancing on trestles? It was a nightmare."

Fact File costs as of August 2002

NAMES: Anne and Robert Waterfall

PROFESSIONS: Retired farmers

AREA: Leicestershire

HOUSE TYPE: Reclaimed brick and stone farmhouse

HOUSE SIZE: 223m²

BUILD ROUTE: Self managed

CONSTRUCTION: Brick and block

FINANCE: Private

BUILD TIME: March '99 – March '01

LAND COST: already owned (est £70,000)

BUILD COST: £110,000

TOTAL COST: £180,000

HOUSE VALUE: £550,000

COST/m²: £493

67% COST SAVING

To create ▶
more character
to the first floor,
the Waterfalls
chose an arched
doorway into one
of the two guest
rooms.

The house ▶ has been designed to look as if it has been extended over the years.

But the Waterfalls did learn a few useful tricks of the trade: to put a layer of polystyrene round the beams at the point where they enter the wall to prevent plaster cracking when the beams dry out, and to paint sheets of mdf which were fixed between the main beams and joists instead of plaster to avoid the same problem.

The flooring was one of the last major jobs. 3" of polystyrene and 2" of polyurethane were laid, followed by

16mm underfloor heating pipes eight inches apart and in five independently controlled zones, which were stapled to the insulation. A layer of screed was placed on top ready for tiling or carpeting with a special underlay designed specifically for underfloor heating.

Outside, Robert had laid a willow filter bed which consisted of three inches of clean hardcore, a membrane followed by a layer of soil, and willows planted over that so that the roots become embedded in the stonework and act as a natural filter.

"Towards the end everything seemed to happen in a rush," says Anne. "Our nephew was moving into the old farmhouse so we moved into the new one before it was completely finished and lived in the kitchen until the joinery work and decorating was complete.

"Building was a great experience and nowhere near as traumatic as people said it would be," says Anne. "The day we moved in we had a big family dinner of roast beef and Yorkshire pudding to celebrate and it was one of the best meals we had ever had. It was a wonderful way to start life in our new home." ■

Useful Contacts

Architect – Eric Lee: 01332 862884

Windows and doors – AJB Timber
Products: 01509 234695

Heating – HCC: 01400 250572

Kitchen – Style Interiors: 01509 216425

Landscaping and drainage – Ground
Services: 01509 820098

Aga and Sanitaryware – Dochin:
                0116 251 5051

Glazing – Hathern Glass: 01509 646423

Stairs – R.N. Shields Ltd.: 01530 412786

Green oak – North Shropshire Timber:
                01691 610721

Reclaimed Bricks – Cawarden Brick
Company Ltd.:   01889 574006

Fireplace – Mowbray Fireplaces:
                01664 410291

Joinery – Gary Booth: 01332 850294

Roofing – Ladderbridge: 01509 506170

There are ▶ currently just two bedrooms, each with en suite facilities, however, the roofspace above the lounge has potential as a third bedroom.

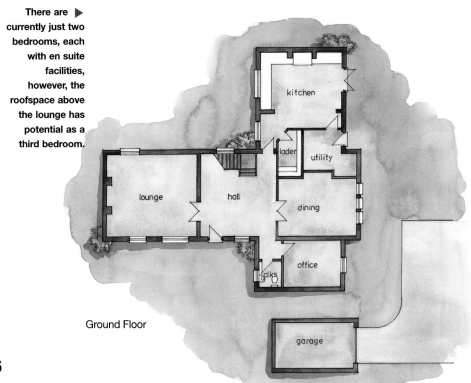

Ground Floor

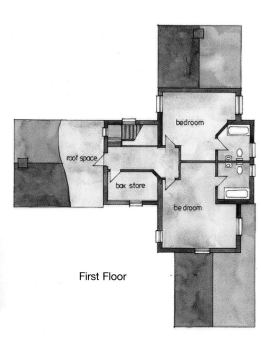

First Floor

DIY Plumbing

Alastair Bruce doesn't claim to be an expert but he's been so successful with doing his own plumbing and UFH that he's now taking on professional jobs. We find out if it can really be that easy.

Alastair Bruce has spent much of his working life on the railways but since taking redundancy he has found that virtually his whole life has revolved around one particular piece of railway land that he was originally called upon to help evaluate.

The land was sold off as surplus to requirements and Alastair used his redundancy money plus some cash from his father to buy it at auction for £45,000, subsequently getting planning permission on it for three houses. For the past two years he's spent his time building two four bedroom houses for resale plus one larger home for himself and his family which is nearing completion. Always fairly handy and a DIY enthusiast, he still had to negotiate a steep learning curve. We asked him about his plumbing and heating experiences.

You say you're a practical person but did you have any previous experience of plumbing?

I've always done things for myself. 20 years ago I put central heating into an old house in Newcastle using second hand radiators and a boiler. It worked. I knew the basics and I got a book out from the library. I didn't have many tools though — only a blowlamp, a pipe cutter and a worm.

Did you design the systems yourself?

For the first two houses I got the name of a plumbing supplier from Exchange & Mart. They did the design for a fee of £40 and then deducted that from the cost of the materials when I ordered them. I didn't follow the plans exactly and I ordered the materials a little late so I had to buy some locally in order to keep

going. Still, the surplus rolled over onto the next house. Those two houses used a vented system with radiators throughout and a normal gas boiler. However, I decided that I wanted underfloor central heating to the ground floor of my own house, using a sealed system with a Combi boiler. I adapted the original designs for the third house but to be honest, it's not brain surgery, especially if you get hold of the information sheets that Wickes put out — they're brilliant. I settled on a Worcester Bosch 'Highflow 400', because I'd extended the central heating in our current house and we'd used one there and been very pleased with it. That one's a gas boiler but the one here will be oil fired. It's the same principle — only at the moment, a lot cheaper to run. People claim that they're not suitable for the larger house but this one has a thermal store. This store feeds the radiators and the hot water, at mains pressure, is drawn off from a coil passing through it. On the whole it works very well. You can run two showers at once but you do need decent water pressure, which we've got around here.

Were you tempted to use the modern plastic plumbing systems?

Not really. I looked into it and whilst I accept that it's a lot easier for those who don't know what they're doing or have never worked with copper, it is more expensive. Of course when it came to the underfloor central heating I used plastic — Thermalfloor 'Unipipe' which is a multi layered plastic/metal pipe. It is clipped in a pattern to re-enforcement mesh within the 70mm screed. It utilises brass manifolds with up to 12 loops coming off each manifold and each loop covering about 18m^2. It's better than just plain plastic because when you bend it, it

stays bent. They give you the patterns but that's not as important as the spacing, which has to be a minimum of 200mm. The longer the run the cooler the water gets so if you want even heat in the room then you lay it out in a coil that goes around the room to the centre and back out again. If you've got a cold spot you lay it out in a zigzag pattern where the hotter pipes start off close to the window. I didn't zone each room — the whole system works off one thermostat.

You've got beam and block floors both upstairs and downstairs, yet you chose to use radiators upstairs.

Yes, I could have had the underfloor upstairs as well but we'd decided we wanted a floating chipboard floor up there and it seemed to make sense to me to use radiators with thermostatic radiator valves. We were having heated towel rails so we had a radiator element up there anyway. I think radiators have their uses. The house is so well insulated that I don't envisage the heating system having to work too hard. We've put attic trusses in and insulated so that we've got a warm roof and I've put all the tails and connections up there for future occupation.

So far I haven't had any major leaks apart from a small dribble on a radiator valve. I think I'm getting quite good. Others must think so, because when I've finished here I'm doing the plumbing and central heating for a client of Design & Materials, the package company I used. ■

> "I adapted the original designs for the third house but to be honest, it's not brain surgery…"

Merry and Ben Albright have built a traditional style oak frame home in just four months thanks to the use of a new construction system. The project was followed for the new series of C4's *Grand Designs*.

Words:
Debbie Jeffery
Photography:
Colin Barratt

Ben and Merry Albright's quaint Herefordshire cottage was built on a tight budget in just four months using structural insulated panels (SIPs).

Pearmain Cottage is the first home for the newly married couple. It is also a first for Border Oak, who designed the small Arts and Crafts style building as a prototype for a new range of houses. The company is well known for its traditional, oak framed homes but decided to offer an alternative: combining oak framing with structural insulated panels to create an ecologically acceptable construction system.

For many self-builders an idyllic country site, affordable budget and fast build time are all dreams which are frequently never realised. Finding building land of any description can prove difficult, whilst over-stretched budgets and prolonged builds are well-known problems. Admittedly, Merry was well placed to find the perfect plot. As the daughter of John Green, founder of Border Oak, she has spent her life amongst architects and builders and is now the company's creative assistant. ▶

A handmade free-standing kitchen from DeVol Kitchens (01509 620 620), with maple and granite worktops and a double Belfast sink, perfectly suits the cottage style.

Instant Character
Building an oak framed cottage in just four months

"When Ben and I first married we lived with my parents, converting an old workshop in their garden," says Merry. "We stayed there while we searched for a plot, which took over a year. Although Border Oak buys and sells land to self-builders everything was simply too expensive. We began to worry that we would never be able to afford to get onto the housing ladder, and started to look around at properties instead."

Finally a suitable piece of land became available in the picturesque Herefordshire village of Pembridge. Border Oak was seeking planning permission for two properties on an old orchard, but the planners preferred the idea of four smaller houses. A compromise was reached: two larger houses would be built, with a third cottage constructed to one side and allocated to a local couple. Merry and Ben decided that this perfectly suited their requirements and purchased the land for £55,000.

The plot is situated in a Conservation Area, in close proximity to a number of listed buildings, which dictated a sensitive design. Planning permission took some time to secure, but was eventually granted for a simple cottage-style dwelling. "I had spent so long talking to other people about their house designs that it took only ten minutes to draw up our own plans," explains Merry. "Ironically, the hardest part had been choosing the type of house we would build, which worked to our advantage as Border Oak was developing a new Arts and Crafts range, and the SIPs idea was being discussed. We decided that we would like to take the opportunity to experiment by combining the two."

The couple restricted the size of their new home to just 130m^2, which could be built using a system of 2½ oak bays. A ground floor sitting room and kitchen are divided by the central hallway, with a weatherboarded utility wing constructed to the west elevation. Upstairs, three bedrooms and two bathrooms benefit from beamed, sloping ceilings and dormer windows. The oak framed porch is a notable feature, with reclaimed and ecologically benign

"Merry e-mailed the TV programme *Grand Designs* and was invited to take part… 'we wanted to show the viewers that self-building does not always end in disaster.'"

Although the ▶ house is clad in SIPs panels, the oak frame structure remains on show inside.

materials used wherever possible. "We were determined not to scrimp on quality," says Ben, "preferring to build a smaller, craftsman-made house without cutting corners. We knew that our money would go further if we kept the cottage relatively modest."

"The oak frame provides the skeleton — a bit like two towers with all the arched braces," continues Merry. "These sit just inside the perimeter of the foundations, with the 142mm SIP panel system constructed outside of these in just three days. Breather membrane was fixed to the outside of the panels and 50mm woodwool slabs on battens provide the key for the traditional lime, sand and horsehair render. This is applied in four coats and wrapped in hessian overnight to prevent it drying out too quickly. Once the roof is on you can work inside and outside the building simultaneously — which folds the build programme in half. The plastering is happening at the same time as the rendering." ▶

▲The French limestone fireplace in the sitting room was made to Merry's own design.

91

The house benefits from underfloor heating supplied by Rehau (0121 344 2300).

A SIP is a building panel made from two facing sheets – generally oriented strand board (OSB) – adhesively welded to a rigid foam core. This effectively turns the panel into an I-beam (similar to a steel joist), providing enormous strength. Full height panels are custom produced under factory conditions, with apertures left for windows and doors. These are delivered to site, slotted together and nailed into position when a conventional outer leaf of brickwork, weatherboarding or tile can be added. Combining an oak frame with the SIPs system provides the best of both worlds – an attractive visible internal structural frame and one of the most efficient construction systems available.

Merry had e-mailed the television programme *Grand Designs* to let them know about the unusual project, and was invited to take part in the series. "We were extremely excited about the whole idea," she explains. "Perhaps we would have been concerned if we had been less knowledgeable about the build process and what it would entail, but we wanted to show the viewers that self-building does not always end in disaster.

> "Merry decided to take advantage of the connection with Grand Designs… 'Madam, everybody says that,' was the disbelieving response."

"So many of these programmes seem to focus on the negative aspects of a project as this makes far more interesting viewing – but ours took just four months to complete, which meant that the cameras could show the entire process from beginning to end. There will be no need to revisit us in six months time for an update because everything was in place. It took 12 weeks to build, with Border Oak completing all of the work from clearing the site to supplying and fitting the doors, windows, oak flooring and staircase. Ben and I then spent a further four weeks organising the bathrooms, kitchen and decorating."

The build was slightly delayed when an old well was discovered on the site. It was necessary to excavate the land by over one metre in order to reduce the impact of the new cottage on its surroundings, and an archaeological survey was one of the planning conditions – costing the Albrights more than £2,000. "It was an unexpected expense," says Ben, who helped to erect the oak framing and SIPs panels. "A local company was instructed and discovered a hearth from a mediaeval cottage, a collection of smoking pipes and a 17th century pot. The stone well was unearthed on the driveway, and has been filled in and preserved for future archaeologists to find – together with Merry's digital camera and two pairs of glasses she lost!"

Further delays were incurred when the couple could not get British Telecom to visit their site for several months. Merry decided to take advantage of the connection with *Grand Designs*, mentioning that the build was being filmed for Channel 4 and that it was in BT's own interests to attend. "Madam, everybody says that," was the disbelieving response. Apparently self-builders have cottoned on to the advantages of being TV stars!

Ben and Merry's friends and family helped them throughout the build. "The house is so much better than we could ever have dreamed, and we feel incredibly lucky to have been able to work with so many talented craftsmen and friends," says Ben. "Some of the carpenters have known Merry since she was a little girl, and the cottage incorporates a number of extremely personal touches - with detailing copied from the school where we met and the lychgate at the church where we married. Wherever we live in the future our first home will always be particularly special. It has been a really exciting few months." ∎

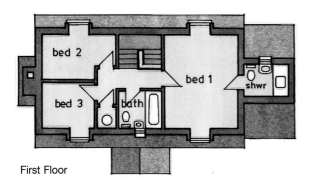

First Floor

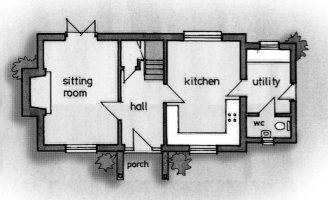

Ground Floor

FLOORPLAN: The simple floorplan allowed the three bedroom cottage to be built using 2 ½ oak bays, with the ground floor kitchen and sitting room separated by a central entrance hall.

Fact File costs as of April 2003

NAMES: Ben and Merry Albright

PROFESSIONS: Economic Development Officer, and Creative Assistant at Border Oak

AREA: Herefordshire

HOUSE TYPE: 3 bedroom cottage

HOUSE SIZE: 130m^2

BUILD ROUTE: Border Oak Package

CONSTRUCTION: Oak frame structure with structural insulated panel (SIP) walls

WARRANTY: Architect's Certificate

FINANCE: Norwich and Peterborough

BUILD TIME: 16 weeks

LAND COST: £55,000
BUILD COST: £85,000
TOTAL COST: £140,000

53% COST SAVING

HOUSE VALUE: £300,000

COST/m^2: £654

Cost Breakdown:
Archaeology, site clearance etc .£4,000
Architect's Certificate £500
Main house package £55,000
Kitchen and utility £8,000
Bathrooms £1,500
Plumbing and underfloor heating .£6,100
Electrics £3,520
Copper guttering £600
Decoration £1,100
Miscellaneous £4,700

TOTAL   **£85,020**

USEFUL CONTACTS: **Design and build package** – Border Oak Design & Construction Ltd: 01568 708 752; **Concrete** – Tarmac Western: 01544 231 029; **Bricks** – York Handmade Brick Company: 01909 540 680; **Foil insulation and breather membrane** – YBS: 01909 721 662; **Breather membrane** - Kingspan Insulation Ltd: 01544 388 601; **Underfloor heating** – Rehau: 0121 344 2300; **Blacksmith** – Bromley O'Hare: 01544 388 645; **Kitchen and utility** – DeVol Kitchens: 01509 620 620; **Copper guttering** – Good Directions Ltd: 01489 577 828; **Paint** – David Oliver Paint Library Ltd: 0207 823 7755; **Sanitaryware** – Albion Bath Co: 01206 794462; Samuel Heath: 0800 0191 282; Waterfront: 0121 520 5346; **Shower doors and trays** - Showerlux: 0247 6639 400 **Lighting** – Byblos: 08700 116 911; **Frosted glass films** – Brume: 020 7737 0670; **Garden design** – Gilly Poultney: 01886 82 2000; **Turf** – Easy Lawn: 01432 850850; **Oven** - Smeg: 0870 990 9907; **Electrical appliances** - Robertsons Electrics: 0800 052 1425

"An individual home for just £32,000!"

Tony Everett explains how he and wife
Tracey built their pretty three bedroom
cottage in Norfolk on a DIY basis,
saving a fortune in the process.

Compiled by: **Jason Orme**
Photography: **Jeremy Pembrey**

My wife Tracey and I knocked around our first home to such an extent that we made enough money on it to be able to seriously consider building our own home. It was something I'd always wanted to do – building's the family business – but I never thought I'd actually get around to it.

Having been the main contractor on other people's self-builds, I'd learned a lot about what worked and didn't – and what were the fundamentals of a good house. With a growing family we had the impetus to really think about our living arrangements and as we're both young – I'm 31 and Tracey's 28 – we knew that we'd be in a great position to put into practice everything I'd learned.

One of the things that held us back initially was that it's increasingly difficult to find good building plots in Norfolk and when we finally heard about one in a nearby village we couldn't believe our luck. However, it still took two or three looks to convince us that it was right.

The site was formed from the sold-off front garden of a neighbour's large bungalow and we thought that it might be a bit too small. It looked pokey and we didn't want to compromise our new home for the sake of rushing to snap up land, but when we saw the outline plans for the plot, any doubts disappeared. We wouldn't get a massive garden but we would get the home we had always wanted.

Remarkably, the plans that were already in place for the plot were just what we had in mind. There were, of course, one or two minor amendments to make the home truly ours – that's the beauty of self-build – but we had the basics of a decent design to work with and bought the plot ▶

▲ The modest sized dining room looks on to the garden, which we're looking forward to seeing develop over the coming years.

for £19,000. The very reasons we were unsure about the plot were what made it so cheap. People were put off by the size, but we had the imagination.

In addition to the bonus of finding a perfect plot — on the main street through a very desirable village — we inherited 6,000 facing bricks, which we found tucked away in the overgrown front hedge, to get us on our way. From that stage on, scheduling was the first and last thing on my mind. Having seen so many people's projects go wrong along the way I knew that with mine, to keep costs down and avoid catastrophes, I'd plan everything down to the last detail. It succeeded — the final cost came to just £100 over budget.

"I'd plan everything down to the last detail. It succeeded — the final cost came to just £100 over budget."

The oak beams ▶ provide an elegant feature in the living room — particularly in the bay, which was an idea from our carpenter.

I spent night after night on our old kitchen table visualising the house down to the position of the furniture, so that when it came to the wiring I wouldn't have any nasty surprises. To finish off the preparation I drew up my own building regulations drawings and did the final amendments to the plans — to change the glass roof on the conservatory to a tile roof, as the conservatory would be north facing and consequently too cold in winter.

What with all the preliminary planning we couldn't wait to finally get stuck in to the build itself. During the winter months we cleared the site — first thing was to build a bridge over the trench at the entrance to the site so that ▶

Bed House for £134,000

wasn't in the trade, so, as I used to be an electrician, I got some headed paper printed and represented myself as an electrical contractor. That did the trick. The trouble was, when it came to the VAT reclaim, I had some tricky questions from the Excise. But they accepted my explanation and it all got sorted out in the end."

They subbed out the plumbing labour but bought all of the materials themselves. They opted for underfloor central heating throughout with 12 separate zones fired by a condensing boiler. "The plumber just walked in on the job one day and asked if we were looking for a plumber," Frank recalls. "We also engaged a local plasterer and the carpenter was a local guy I knew who came in after the first one just disappeared after hanging a few doors. The PVC-u windows and doors came from a local company. The fitting was in the builder's price but they preferred to fit themselves and they gave us a reasonable price to do so, and we deducted that from the builder's price.

"We're happy and proud of our achievement," Frank says. "The total costs, including land, were £189,000 to set against a recent valuation of £245,000. Not bad, and suitable recompense for all those months of hard work and disruption." ∎

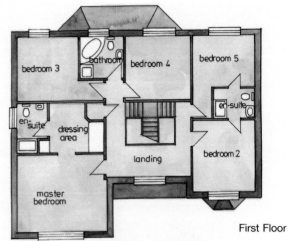

First Floor

Ground Floor

Fact File costs as of february 2003

NAMES: Frank and Emma McCarthy

PROFESSIONS: Fireman and student

AREA: Wales

HOUSE TYPE: Five bed detached

HOUSE SIZE: 320m² + attic

BUILD ROUTE: Builder to shell stage and then DIY/subbies

CONSTRUCTION: MAsonry and brick

FINANCE: Private

BUILD TIME: March '00 – Oct '01

LAND COST: £55,000

BUILD COST: £133,979

TOTAL COST: £188,979	**23%**
HOUSE VALUE: £245,000	**COST**
COST/m²: £418 (exc. attic)	**SAVING**

Cost Breakdown:

Materials	£69,099
Builder	£42,500
Supply and fix kitchen	£4,000
Supply of windows	£4,000
Fix of windows	£300
Odd labour	£1,280
Plasterer	£6,000
Carpenters	£3,000
Plumber	£1,200
Architectural work	£1,900
TOTAL	**£133,979**

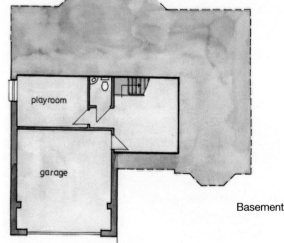

Basement

USEFUL CONTACTS: **Kitchen** – World of Kitchens: 01633 430888; **Doors** – Cardiff Door Centre: 02920 4555534; **Builder** – Wentworth Construction: 01633 431445; **Designer** – Frank Granville, FG Design: 01291 624366

DIY Wiring

Martin Atkins decided to do the first fix wiring in his new home in Braemar himself, saving £2,000. We asked him how he approached a trade that many would be afraid to take on.

Martin and Sally Atkins are building their own 160m² timber frame home in Braemar, site of the famous Highland Games. It's a three bedroom property which emulates a traditional Scottish house and the couple are delighted to be able to tell how, when the inspector from the local electricity board came to visit, he thought that they were actually engaged in a renovation project.

Living in Aberdeen, forty miles away from their site, Martin and Sally can visit and work on the project only at weekends and holidays but they've still managed to do all the plumbing, wiring and plasterboarding themselves. We spoke to them principally about their experiences in doing their own wiring, at an estimated saving of £2,000.

Was this a trade that you'd always planned to do yourselves?

Yes. We'd always planned to do most of the internal fitting out and decorating ourselves and it made sense to be able to do most things at our own pace. If we'd used subcontractors, I would have felt that we had to be here on a daily basis and that just wasn't possible. We've not only saved money by doing things ourselves – it's eased our cashflow and means that if we want to change things midstream then we can do so without upsetting anyone. If I make a mistake then it's my own fault. I have had previous experience of re-wiring a house but it was nearly 25 years ago. That was it before I took on this task.

Did you read much in order to learn what to do?

I read a Collins DIY manual and the guide to IEEE regulations, available from any electrical supplier. I kept things simple but I reckon that anyone who can wire up a plug and understands the basics would be able to do this. Of course, to fill in the application forms for the supply you have to have a registered electrician down as the main contractor. I got a local guy from the village, who had given me a price but wasn't able to fit the work in. I was able to talk to him about a few things before I started.

The only equipment I had to buy was a voltmeter and a Martindale socket tester. We're hooked up to the mains now through the temporary supply that was brought into the meter box. It comes into the electronic meter and you wire up your own consumer unit. That's not as hair raising as it sounds — modern equipment has a switch on the meter than isolates the supply and there's little danger with Residual Current Devices.

You say you kept things simple but surely you've put in some special things to individualise your home?

No, not really. We've got a separate ring main for the power and lighting both upstairs and downstairs. There's also some floor sockets, concealed lighting in the inglenook and plenty of outside lights on Passive Infrared Detectors. We've got smoke alarms in most rooms with heat detectors in the garage, kitchen and boiler room. I expect that if they all went off the noise would be indescribable.

I did consider 12 volt lighting but felt that the installation costs were rather expensive and I wanted to keep things simple. Most of the lights will be fitted with halogen bulbs anyway.

The major difficulty I've had is working out what circuits to install and where to drill holes in the timber frame to minimise the runs and avoid weakening the structure. Although this is a timber frame, there is a lot of steel in the construction and Murphy's Law always dictates that the steel is where you need to run. I thought that the cooker cable would be dead easy but in the end I had to divert around steel to get to the position. We'd allowed voids and service ducts in the original plans but they weren't sufficient.

Will the same electrician certify the installation for you?

I hope so. That's been my main worry, especially as an electrician who is working for us at home tells me that his association frown on people doing their own work. I reckon there's an element of sour grapes because it's just so easy when it comes down to it.

All in all, it hasn't been a difficult trade to carry out. I've taken it steadily and if I've been unsure of something I've taken the time to find out about it. Planning how you approach the runs is the key — once you've worked that out, it's simply a matter of unrolling the cable and getting on with it.

We're not quite finished but the part of the system that's up and running seems to be doing well. I've no reason to suppose that the complete installation will pose any major problems. ■

"I reckon that anyone who can wire a plug and understands the basics would be able to do this…"

Perfectly Planned

A spacious new family home built for just £67,000

Jon and Cath Gribble completed their new three bedroomed family home near Halifax on time and on budget thanks to meticulous forward planning.

"The biggest decision in any self-build project is to stop the talking and actually go ahead and do it," advises Jon Gribble, who not long after having taken his own advice, found himself with no job, no home and, despite two years of searching, still no building plot. Fortunately, he recounts this particular episode in his life with good humour, because not long afterwards, his luck turned for the better.

Jon and wife Cath had sold their two bedroomed semi in Bradford, West Yorkshire, in the spring of 1998 in readiness to buy a plot and had moved in with Cath's parents "for a couple of months". Their plans to build themselves a new home began to look a little hasty when Jon was unexpectedly made redundant, but what may have seemed like a disaster at the time ultimately did nothing more than delay their plans. Jon was only out of work for four weeks and the discovery of a new job was followed by another more important find — a building plot in the district of Shelf on the outskirts of Halifax.

"We saw the land advertised in the paper on a Saturday, made an offer on the Monday morning at 9.00am and by lunchtime the offer was accepted," recalls Jon. Before he and Cath could proceed with the purchase, however, they needed to show their mortgage lender exactly what they were going to build for valuation purposes and that meant convincing the vendor to wait for several weeks whilst they applied for detailed planning permission.

"Thankfully, the vendor agreed," says Jon, who risked several hundred pounds in design fees and on a site survey to assess the ground conditions, long before the deal was secured by the exchange of contracts.

Fortunately, no one objected to the application and by May bank holiday 1999, with planning and their mortgage finally in place, the sale of the land was completed. Jon wasted no time in getting started and immediately began putting up fences and clearing the site. "After such a long wait, it was fantastic to finally know the plot was ours," he says. What Jon recalls as probably the best moment of the project was followed only a week later by the worst.

Whilst waiting for the planners to cast their decision, Jon and Cath had been busy working out a detailed budget for every stage of a build which they knew would stretch their finances to the very limit. Fortunately, that budget included a ten per cent contingency sum, because no sooner had they started excavating the trenches for the footings, than the ground swallowed up almost every penny of it.

"We had dug trial holes as part of the site survey to find out what sort of foundations we would need," explains Jon. "They had suggested we need dig down only 0.7m and so when the inspectors from the NHBC and the local authority told us they wanted us to go down 2.5m it was a nasty shock. The site survey had failed to account for the spread of the roots of a neighbour's willow tree."

As if this was not trouble enough, the digger then uncovered a disused cesspit left over from a 19th century school house. "The trial holes had missed it by less than 0.5m," says Jon. "The only solution was to dig it out and fill the hole with concrete." Fortunately, the digger bucket hit bedrock at 2.2m, but nonetheless, the cost of the footings had more than doubled from their estimate. ▶

◀ The windows – including this feature arched window in the hall which overlooks Shelf – were made by a local carpenter in hardwood for less than the price of softwood from leading suppliers.

Words:
Michael Holmes
Photography:
Jeremy Phillips

105

The slate flooring in the kitchen is from Wickes. The kitchen units were an end of line bargain from Do It All. ▶

"The two bricklayers we had retained to build the shell of the house were very philosophical about it all," recalls Jon. "They explained that the one cost that no one can predict on a new house is the foundations. They were still adamant, however, that they could build the shell for the price they had quoted, and in just eight weeks. This was a great comfort to hear and they were as good as their word, finishing with a week to spare."

Whilst the shell was going up, Jon started interviewing plumbers, electricians, carpenters and plasterers in readiness to progress the first fix. Meanwhile, Cath was in charge of finding the best possible deals on all of the fixtures and fittings. "We bought the kitchen from Focus Do It All before we had even finalised the site and put it into storage at a friend's warehouse," recalls Jon. "It was an end of line bargain and too good a deal to miss.

"You can't rely on deals coming up just when you need them... the trick is to be on the look out all the time."

"We also saved a lot of money by buying things at liquidation sales, like our bathrooms. You can't rely on deals coming up just when you need them and so the trick is to be on the look out all the time and be ready to buy things when you see them – providing you have got the funds that is. In our case, we worked out that cashflow was going to be pretty tight during the build and at one point, it looked like this might make it impossible for us to build. Then I saw an advert for the Accelerator mortgage from BuildStore which lends 95% on land and releases the stage payments in advance. It cost only about the same as a conventional stage payment mortgage which releases funds in arrears and was just what we needed."

Thanks to their careful forward planning, the remainder of the project went very smoothly. Each of the trades were hired on a fixed price and deadline, with the details agreed in a formal letter. "The subbies were all used to working on nothing more than a verbal agreement and were a bit suspicious of a formal letter at first," says Jon. "But in the end I think they appreciated it, because everyone knew where they stood." ▶

Useful Contacts

Cast Stone - Darlstone, Natural Stone Products Ltd: 01624 897916

Cast Stone Slates - Naylor Roof Slates, Denby Dale Cast Stone Quarries: 01484 863560

Architectural Masonry - Ibstock: 01530 261999

Merchant - Naylor Myers: 01484 712531

Timber - CR Taylor: 01274 832 912

Structural Guarantee - NHBC Solo for Self Build: 01494 735760

Accelerator Mortgage - BuildStore: 0870 8709991

Slate Flooring - Wickes: 0500 300328

Combi Boiler - Ocean Alpha Combi Max: 01332 613924

Plumber & Electrician – BM Services: 01274 851455

...n and Cath are very proud
...heir new home – which is
...n infinitely better quality
...n offered by developers.

"The couple moved in less than six months after starting on site and just £7,000 over their original budget…"

Jon managed the building work and kept all of the tradesmen supplied with materials. "You have to visit every day, even if only for five minutes," he says. "Not to crack the whip, but to have a chat and see how they are getting on and to let them know you are there, keeping an eye on progress and quality."

As soon as the plasterer had completed the ground floor rooms, Jon started working on the house himself. Together with his father and his father in law, he laid the floors, hung the doors, fitted the skirting and architrave, kitchen and bathrooms, did all of the decorating and laid the drive.

"There was a lot of family input in this build for which we are very grateful," says Jon. "I worked around twenty hours every weekend on the house, plus a couple of hours every night after work, and more towards the end of the project when we had set a deadline for moving in – we had to let Cath's parents have their house back sometime. We ended up living there for eighteen months!"

The couple moved in early in November 1999, less than six months after starting on site and just £7,000 over their original budget, including the cost of the garage which Jon says they had not really intended to build.

"We didn't think we had the money to build the garage straightaway," says Jon. "However, when the builders started on site they dug out the footings for the garage too and I decided just to let them carry on. I kind of turned a blind eye to it – an odd approach I know, considering how meticulously we planned and managed the rest of the build, but I reckoned we could wing it, and I was right."

Jon, Cath and their two young children are all delighted with their new home, which the couple say they could never have afforded had they not self-built. Jon's only regret is that they used preformed roof trusses which now prevent them from converting the attic space. "However, I always come to the conclusion that this was not an option." he says. "We had committed our budget and we simply could not have afforded the extra cost. Maybe next time though, because we will definitely build again." ∎

Fact File costs as of March 2002

NAME: Jon and Cath Gribble

PROFESSION: Sales Engineer & Part-time Customer Adviser

AREA: Halifax, West Yorkshire

HOUSE TYPE: Three bed detached

HOUSE SIZE: 144m²

BUILD ROUTE: Self-managed subcontractors plus DIY

CONSTRUCTION: Insulated blockwork cavity walls with recon stone cladding

WARRANTY: NHBC Solo for Self Build

SAP RATING: 87

FINANCE: BuildStore Accelerator

BUILD TIME: June '98 – Nov '99

LAND COST: £40,750	
BUILD COST: £67,000	**26%**
TOTAL COST: £107,750	**COST SAVING**
HOUSE VALUE: £145,000	
COST/m²: £465	

Cost Breakdown:

Foundations	£7,000
Weathertight Shell	£36,000
Plaster	£3,000
First Fix	£2,300
Second Fix	£2,900
Kitchen	£2,500
Bathroom	£1,500
Plumbing & Electrics	£5,000
Fees and services	£6,800
TOTAL	**£67,000**

◀ **Jon and Cath designed the layout of the house themselves, using the services of a designer purely to produce working drawings and to handle the planning application.**

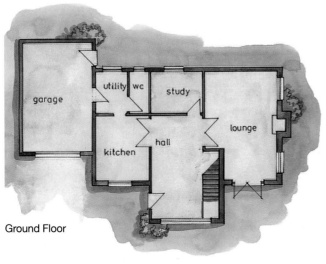

Ground Floor

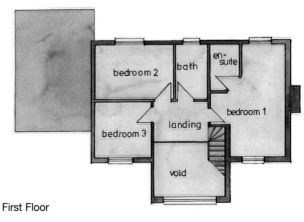

First Floor

DIY Wall Finishes

Adrian Cooper's a bit of a DIY fanatic — much to the despair of long suffering wife Carole. We talked to him about the daunting task of doing your own plastering and gained some handy tips.

Adrian Cooper's no stranger to DIY — he's tried his hand at nearly every trade over the years. He's never built a house from scratch, however, and his wife Carole's glad of that. "He'd want to do everything himself and that would be a nightmare," she explains. "I don't mind helping out with renovations, where we can live in the house during work, but I wouldn't want to have to put our lives on hold."

Their latest project is the renovation of a three bedroom detached house in Surrey. The property needed quite a bit of attention and had scope for extension as well as general updating. Carole's mum has come to stay with the family so as well as adding two extra bedrooms within the house, they are converting the garage to provide 'granny flat' accommodation. They paid £125,000 for the original house and have spent £10–15,000 on it, doing most of the work themselves. They have recently had it valued at £230,000, with more to come when the annexe is completed — so it's been more than worth their while. However, what H&R wanted to talk about specifically was Adrian's experiences of doing his own plastering.

Plastering is the one trade that most people will not attempt, yet you are quite relaxed about it.

I don't do ceilings! As for walls, about 25 years ago I bought a house cheap because it had wet rot. As part of the job of restoring it, I had to hack the plaster off the walls to about 1m high in all of the rooms. I couldn't afford a professional to do the replastering, so it became a baptism of fire. I rendered and set it using Carlite Browning & Bonding with a finish coat. It wasn't perfect but I got better. It took me quite a while to realise that plaster has a very limited shelf life. The plaster kept going off in the bucket. Then a mate came with me to the merchants and he climbed up on the pile of bags and picked some out by their date. From then on it got better and I've never had the same problem since.

So did you render and set here?

No, the first rooms I did were the two new bedrooms and, as Carole was about to move in, I had to get the rooms decorated quickly so chose to dry line them — not an ideal choice. I used taper edge boarding and then filled and sanded the joints. Despite being very quick to dry, it was messy — there was dust everywhere.

In the next rooms, I tacked, taped and skim coated the walls using butt edged boards. Even though wet plaster is messy, it's easier to contain the mess in one room and put down sheets or covers. I tacked onto wooden studs and taped the joints with a sticky back scrim (Fibretape). That was terrific — it was so much easier than dry lining, having to sandwich silk scrim between wet plaster.

It's all in the mix, they say...

Absolutely right, the mixture is everything. It should be the consistency of whipped cream — use an electric drill with a mixer attach-ment. The other important thing is to never add water to plaster. Add the plaster to the water, mixing as you go. It might mean ending up with too much or not enough water but don't be tempted to add more, it won't work. Use clean buckets and a clean spot board set on a trestle so you don't have to keep bending to load the hawk.

Apply the mix over the wall to about 3mm thickness, smoothing it as much as possible but not to a finish. Leave it for 20 minutes before going back on it with water and a clean float to iron out the high spots and trowel marks. Make sure you have plenty of clean water for this stage. Others recommend using a large paintbrush to flick the water onto the surface but I find that a hand held spray is less messy. Always trowel at a slight angle, pushing it in a semi-circular movement, flicking water ahead of you as you iron out the ridges and fill in the hollows. Keep cleaning the trowel off or

"Try your technique on smaller areas first. Don't panic or be too fussy...."

the build up of plaster on the trailing edge will drag the plaster.

So do you think that people should try a whole wall on their first attempt?

No, try your technique on smaller areas first. Don't panic and don't try to be too fussy. When I first started I'd get pretty good then try to get it just a little bit better and muck it all up. If needs be, let it dry then fill it or rub it down later rather than keep on trying to work plaster that's gone off.

Does that also apply to render and set?

The initial training I got with render and set was good as I was working to a guide. If you are worried, you could tack battens and render to them but the finish has to be freehand. I've done sand and cement render but mostly used Bonding or Browning. Browning has to dry thoroughly before it is finished, probably after a coat of Unibond. Bonding can be finished when touch dry. I'm intending to use Fermacell boards and finish in the granny annexe. By the end of all of this I reckon I'll really be an expert in wall finishes! ∎

A stunning site combined with real life drama means that Bill and Kay Thornton's new self-built home has a tremendous sense of place.

Words: **Jason Orme**   Photography: **Geoff Harris**

Magazines, exhibitions and, most of all, real life self-builders will happily declare the overriding sense of satisfaction and life affirming nature of building your own home. Nobody will agree with them more than Kay Thornton, who along with husband Bill is now living in a stylish self-built house in a prominent position over-looking Morecambe Bay. The fact that she spent one morning celebrating gaining planning approval only to spend the afternoon coming to terms with the news that a brain tumour would give her months to live, means that their new home is an achievement and monument in its own right.

When the native Lancastrians decided to retire back to Morecambe after a hectic life working in the oil industry, they spent months looking for a very simple thing – the right house in the right area. "But it wasn't forthcoming," explains Bill, "and when a friend up here mentioned that, of all things, he'd just bought some land to build a house on, it seemed like the ideal solution to our problem."

"We were driving on the main coastal road out of Morecambe when we came across a piece of land that must have just gone up for sale that day," says Bill. "We bought it pretty much right away. We saw the potential." And what potential. A sloping plot with what could well be spectacular sea views. "It wasn't that obvious," he contin ▶

The first floor ▶
living room (ABOVE THE CARPORT) is strategically placed to make the most of views over Morecambe Bay.

A GREAT PERSPECTIVE

A new house designed to make the most of elevated views

"We needed extra deep foundations owing to the fact that we were next to a railway line…"

▲ The spacious hallway gives a real sense of architectural worth and is the one real example of space for space's sake — the rest of the rooms are of modest proportions.

continues. "The slope down to the sea was such that the view would be blocked out without clever design. We knew that if we could build a house that was high enough out of the ground, we could just about manage it."

A few weeks spent sounding out potential builders proved fruitful. "We talked to lots of builders, none of whom could give us anything like a fixed price," he says. "Money would have to be well managed – this was our retirement project – and we needed to know where we stood. Thankfully through some local contacts, we met Steven White who gave us confidence in him. I was going to project manage the site initially, although after meeting him I felt he'd be able to do a better job."

On a site with such great potential, it was vital to make sure the house would do it justice. "Forward planning was

of paramount importance to the design," explains Kay. "All of us spent time balancing precariously on ladders to see if we could get the right view from the main living areas. We knew that the sea view to the west would be important to us, but there were also some fabulous views to the south over Lancaster. The elevated position really brought out the best in the designer."

At this stage most self-builders face a crucial decision – timber frame or brick and block construction? The Thorntons came up with a Third Way – to use both. "We knew we wanted the living area to be on one floor but if we'd gone for pure timber frame, the elevations would not have been enough," explains Bill. "As a result we decided to construct a base from brick and block and pop the timber frame – from Maple Timber Frame – on top. The site proved problematical in two ways. We needed extra deep foundations owing to the fact that we were next to a railway line and British Rail Property Board wanted assurances that we wouldn't be damaging the embankment;

and the slope meant that, with having to build up the west side of the house, we had to use steel supports as rafts."

Planning permission came easily thanks to a sympathetic design in the local vernacular – "we had no choice in the render," explains Bill – but when approval came, the bombshell of Kay's life threatening illness shook the couple to their foundations. "I wanted to give up," says Bill. "Nothing else mattered but Kay. But she insisted on the house continuing, if only to give me something to focus on apart from the traumas. We took time away – the builders were excellent in this respect – and then, remarkably, Kay didn't deteriorate as expected. And as the house began to rise out of the ground, she began to recover. And within a month of an operation she was sweeping up after the builders."

For weeks the fortress-like site gave up nothing in the way of clues to passers by about what lay within. Then, from behind the six foot hedges, the timber frame went on and the potential began to be realised. "Kay was busy

planning the interiors, while I was on site labouring," says Bill.

Kay and Bill's layout, based on a range of designs from Ian Gibson that eventually came to fruition through Maple Timber Frame, decreed that every room in the house had to have an aspect and a function. An imposing hall and wheelchair access were necessary. They will be the first to admit that the floorplan is far from revolutionary, but every room takes full advantage of the position. Kay can enjoy watching the rabbits in a neighbouring field whilst doing the dishes and the guest bedrooms still enjoy sea views – yet the real treat lies in the informal sitting room, where visitors are treated to a spectacular view over the Bay. "We spend hours in here, obviously," says Bill. "We enjoy watching the range of wildlife and at night, greatly enjoy watching the lights of Grange over Sands twinkle in the distance. We have some outstanding sunsets up here and that view really is the raison d'etre of the whole house."

▲ On a clear day the kitchen has a stunning view over the Lancashire coast all the way down to Blackpool Tower.

▶

The rear elevation shows how the levels work, with the main living area on the first floor, and integral garage (TO THE RIGHT, WITHOUT WINDOWS) and car port to the left.

Fact File costs as of September 2001

NAME: Bill and Kay Thornton

PROFESSIONS: Retired

AREA: Lancashire

HOUSE TYPE: Single storey elevated to two storeys at rear and west

HOUSE SIZE: 204m²

BUILD ROUTE: Builder as main contractor

CONSTRUCTION: Brick and block and timber frame

WARRANTY: Architect's certificate

SAP RATING: Not known

FINANCE: Private

BUILD TIME: August '96 – April '97

LAND COST: £55,000

BUILD COST: £86,240

TOTAL COST: £141,240

CURRENT VALUE: £275,000

49% COST SAVING

COST/M²: £422

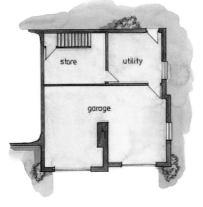

Lower Ground Floor

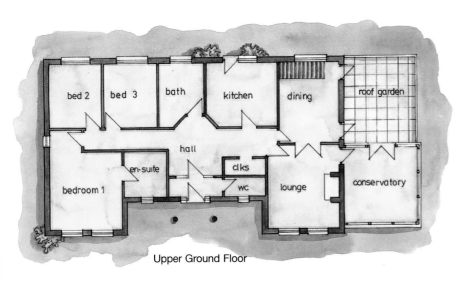

Upper Ground Floor

Whilst the house certainly realises the potential of the site, Bill and Kay have left plenty of scope for further improvement. "We specified attic trusses so that the loft can be used for living space should future occupants desire, and the basement level, which we use for storage and garage space, could easily be used as living accommodation as we've also got a car port under the jettying living room. But we don't need the room right now."

Bill and Kay's story is remarkable in many ways. "Owing to the rather prominent location we get a great amount of sightseers," says Bill. "It's strange to think that people actually point and stare and take photos of our house from the road – probably thanks to the elevated living room – and we've had a few unwarranted visitors asking us if we'd like to sell. We're not!" What makes it a truly incredible story is the way that Bill and Kay, in the face of very grim reality, have created something that transcends even that – evidence surely that building your own home is about so much more than saving money. ■

Useful Contacts

Timber Frame — Maple Timber Frame: 01772 683370

Architect — Ian Gibson at Gill Dockray Architects: 01539 722656

Main Contractor — Steven White at Lunsdale Builders: 01524 823248

Roofing Slates — Modern SM Grey at Marley: 01675 468400

Quoins — Boland Stone (Kendal): 01539 723600

DIY Plastering

Plastering is notorious for being the trade that looks a great deal easier than it really is, but this didn't put off DIY renovator Alan Griffiths. We find out how he got on.

"We've been through all of this before but I sometimes wonder why we do it," says serial renovator Alan Griffiths, in a rare moment of self doubt. For this particular project Alan is taking a tiny two up two down cottage and turning it into a four bedroom family home worth twice what he paid for it. When it is all over, he'll have around 150m² of house with superb views, lots of outbuildings and walled gardens, within which, in a sheltered position, he is determined to have a hot tub!

Alan had done all of the re-wiring, the plumbing, the plastering, the 2nd fix joinery and kitchens himself, as well as the fitting of the new uPVC windows. What we wanted to talk to him about, in particular, was the plastering.

Have you done any plastering before?

I'd never really done plastering on my own before but it's all a matter of confidence. You can over-trowel and you can mess it up, but you can always put it right. I started off doing the sand and cement render and scratch coat. This gives you the right practice and helps you learn the techniques and the right pressures. Don't be frightened of it.

But here you seem to have dry lined in most places.

That's right. I started off gluing the boards on dabs but I got into an awful muddle and I changed to using battens. Then my old mate who is a plasterer by trade came around and saw that it was taking me an awfully long time, so he persuaded me to go back to dabs. I tried putting the dabs on the board but it was uncontrollable and they kept falling off, so I've reverted to putting the dabs on the wall, four lines of five, and then offering up the board to them. My friend lent me his long aluminium straight edge to slap the boards up. If you're putting the boards on vertically then you hold the bottom with your foot and then slap the

edge onto the board and push it home. At first I was getting it wrong and putting too much pressure on the sides. When I slapped the middle, the sides had already compressed and pushed the dabs too far in. The spring in the board then caused loss of adhesion at the edges. I messed around with the boards too much and kept trying to get them right and you can't really do that. You've got to slap them up and leave them or you'll lose all adhesion.

At first, when my friend suggested putting the boards on horizontally, I thought that he was mad and that it would be too difficult to put the top layers of board up and hold them. In fact it's great. You put the bottom board on in the same way that you would if you were putting the boards vertically, only there's not so far to stretch so it's easier to get it right.

You offer the board up to the dabbed wall and then, holding the straight edge with your foot, you slap it against the board and push it on. For the next layer it is in fact easier because, far from being heavy and difficult, you can rest the board on the lower one and then slap it home. The straight edge then lines the joint up with the one below and you don't get any unevenness.

With the boards vertical, you always get a whip in the board and if you're on your own it is uncontrollable. Either way, though, if you do get it wrong you can always take the unevenness out. I've had to do that in a few of the reveals but now that I've got the hang of the dry lining, I won't have to do this.

And then you skim coat it?

Yes. Again, don't be frightened — but watch it like a hawk. As soon as the first coat starts to turn, get the second coat on and then wait for

▲ **"Plastering is all a matter of confidence," says Alan. "You can over-trowel and mess it up, but you can always put it right."**

that to turn before trowelling it off. When it does, go for it, with big swings. If you get it right you don't need too much water. The lumpy bits that hang on the trowel are useful for filling in holes. Trowel in 45° arcs across the wall and if you need to take out the trowel marks, don't go in the same direction. It's best to reverse the swing so that you cross them.

Any other hints to pass on?

The first thing to do is to buy a proper drill bit mixer. Add the powder to the water rather than the other way round and aim for the consistency of thick custard. As for materials, I've found that self adhesive scrim is best for taping up the joints and on ceilings I prefer the ready mixed, textured coating. Getting a smooth finish on ceilings is a really difficult job! ■

"Add the powder to the water, not the other way round... and aim for the consistency of thick custard."

▲ Jacqui designed the pretty cottage interiors herself, using simple natural colours and lots of stained pine.

Damon and Jacqui Holloway's pretty Victorian style cottage in Hampshire is full of traditional character yet didn't cost them a fortune to build.

Jacqui Holloway says she was apprehensive when husband Damon first suggested they build their own home. "I thought of all the complications and the things that could go wrong," she says. "But Damon talked me into it! He saw self-build as a good way of making money and was very confident that we could do it – especially as he knows lots of local tradesmen from his school days."

▶

Words:
Michael Holmes

Pictures:
Nigel Rigden

Traditional

Values

A Victorian style cottage built for only £50,000

French doors ▶ from hall to living room improve the flow of the house and bring light into the hallway which does not have a window.

The Holloways ▶ chose an energy saving wall mounted Gloworm boiler to fire their radiator central heating system and to feed the hot water cylinder in the attic. The compact gas fired boiler is neatly concealed in a kitchen cupboard.

With two growing children, Ben, then aged five, and Amber aged two, the Holloways wanted to move from their three bedroom estate house to a larger property with a big garden. Ironically, whilst house hunting the couple viewed the plot on which they would eventually build – then the garden of the house next door – but failed to spot the potential. "We didn't realise that the garden was big enough to divide up and create a plot," says Jacqui.

The development opportunity did not remain unspotted for long. A speculator snapped up the house for £82,000, quickly obtained outline planning permission for a chalet bungalow in the garden, and then sold both properties on

individually for a healthy profit. Jacqui and Damon realise now that they missed a fantastic opportunity but admit that they had not even considered building until they saw the plot up for sale. "We would have made more money, but we have done very well here anyway," says Jacqui.

The couple started drawing design sketches for a Victorian style cottage and after a visit to the planning office to sound out the chances of building a house rather than a chalet bungalow, agreed to buy the plot for £37,500.

"We designed the house ourselves," says Jacqui. "I started with the kitchen, as I knew exactly what I wanted: a traditional farmhouse style layout with a dining area, a

range style cooker set in a brick inglenook, and a stable door. We also knew that we wanted four bedrooms and two bathrooms. Although we only really needed three, we knew that a fourth bedroom would maximise the value of the house should we ever decide to sell. Above all, we wanted a house that could be lived in, with a country cottage look and a warm and homely feel."

Jacqui and Damon took their sketch ideas along to see local designer David Lloyd. Familiar with local planning policies, David knew what would and would not be acceptable in design terms and helped Damon and Jacqui formulate their ideas. On their next meeting, both parties

"Above all, we wanted a house that could be lived in, with a country cottage look and a warm, homely feel."

found that they had come up with very similar design schemes for a traditional looking brick cottage under a slate roof, with a garage tucked behind and to one side.

"David's service was excellent value," says Jacqui. "He handled the planning application for us as well as the Building Regulations. We experienced no problems with either. Although the outline consent was for a chalet bungalow, the planners were very supportive about us

▲ To keep down costs Damon bought a simple straight flight of stairs, cut it into two sections and built the half landing.

▶

119

◄ Blue glass blocks with mirror backing set into the bathroom walls add to the fun nautical theme in the family bathroom.

changing to a full two storey design. Their only concern was that we should not overlook next door's garden. Consequently, we do not have a window on the landing in the hall, and the window in Amber's room had to have obscured glazing."

Budget was a big factor in the build and to keep down costs Damon decided to manage the building project himself rather than use a main contractor. As a self-employed heating services engineer, he was able to visit the site every day to co-ordinate labour and materials as well as get involved in the work itself.

To fund the purchase of the plot, Damon and Jacqui sold their home and moved in with Damon's parents. They then had just enough money left over to pay their design fees and to get the foundations built. The rest of the money needed to complete the build was borrowed from NatWest bank who later converted the building loan into a fixed rate mortgage once the couple had moved in.

The house is built using traditional cavity wall construction, with aircrete inner blockwork and clad with Michelmersh ATR bricks which Jacqui chose because they looked old and had character. "They were a bit more expensive, but it is a price worth paying, especially as we saved money elsewhere," she says.

The Holloways' primary objective was to create a home with character and so the couple spent a lot of time looking at the many Victorian houses and cottages in the area and researching ideas from magazines. The brickwork detailing is a good example of their endeavours. They have built a brick plinth around the base of the house, run a decorative string course between the ground and first floors, and have created brick arches above the window openings instead of building just flat, characterless soldier courses. Together with white painted top hung timber windows that emulate the look of box sash frames, a carefully cut filigree barge board and a pretty cottage porch, both also in white, the house fits in very well with its century old neighbours.

"We didn't have a fortune to spend, so we had to keep down costs all the way," explains Jacqui. "That is why Damon did a lot himself during evenings and weekends, including all of the electrics; fixing the plasterboard ready for skimming; fitting the stairs; making and fixing the bargeboards and porch; fitting the kitchen and bathrooms; and all of the decorating and landscaping. I would have got more involved myself, but the children were both very young at the time and so I had to look after them."

To ensure that they got the best value from their subcontractors, the couple arranged to get three quotes for each of the trades and shopped around for all of their materials, opening trade accounts with two local builder's merchants. They also managed to find a few bargains,

Fact File costs as of July 2001

NAME: Damon and Jacqui Holloway

PROFESSIONS: Heating Controls Engineer and Part time Customer Services Officer

AREA: Hampshire

HOUSE TYPE: Four bed detached

HOUSE SIZE: 110m²

BUILD ROUTE: Self-managed subcontractors plus DIY

CONSTRUCTION: Brick and block

WARRANTY: Zurich

FINANCE: NatWest

BUILD TIME: June '95 – January '96

LAND COST: £37,500

BUILD COST: £51,434

TOTAL COST: £88,934

CURRENT VALUE: £235,000

COST/M²: £467

68% COST SAVING

Cost Breakdown:

Design Fees	£806
Local Authority Fees	£590
Zurich Warranty	£700
Groundworks/Foundations	£4,288
Service Connections	£1,255
Shell	£13,373
Scaffold hire	£570
Timber (roof, joists & carcassing)	£2,618
Doors, windows & glazing	£2,551
Carpentry	£2,370
Rooftiles	£2,040
Roofing & Felting	£1,100
Plasterboard & Skim	£1,427
Stairs, doors & mouldings	£1,100
Electrics	£420
Plumbing & Heating	£1,910
Bathrooms	£695
Kitchen	£2,894
Flooring	£2,100
Decorating materials	£525
Fencing	£1,100
Landscaping	£2,500
Skips & Labour	£312
Garage	£4,190
TOTAL	**£51,434**

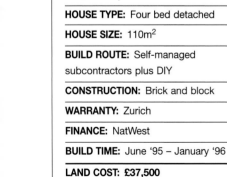

such as the cast iron fireplace in the sitting room which cost only £60 from a junk shop. Reclaimed decorative clay ridge tiles cost just £3.50 each from Romsey Reclamation and the fireplace in the master bedroom was free, as it was recovered from a skip.

"We were very lucky with the build," says Jacqui. "There were no major problems and at the end of the day we got exactly what we wanted. One of the few mistakes we made was in not planning ahead for a potential loft conversion. I would like to make use of the roof space now, but it would entail moving all of the header tanks and Damon is not so keen. He built the garage together with a friend only a couple of years ago — we didn't have the money to build it at the same time as the house — and now he wants a rest for a while from DIY projects. He is currently restoring an old motorcycle out in the garage."

Damon and Jacqui's advice to other self-builders is not to set an unrealistic time schedule. "We originally aimed to be in by Christmas, but didn't actually get finished until January," says Jacqui. "Even then, we had all of the painting to finish and no carpets! It is better to be realistic, especially if you are doing a lot of the work yourself."

Although their total build costs came well within their estimate of £50–55,000, including a VAT refund of £5,005, the couple also warn against setting too tight a budget. "Building your own home will always cost £5–10,000 more than you think," says Jacqui, "there are always extras and finishing touches, so leave a bit of slack."

"Looking back, it was a very satisfying experience," concludes Jacqui. "The house is even better than we hoped and it has also been very financially rewarding. We have really managed to move up the housing ladder by self-building and would definitely consider doing it again — providing we can find another plot not too far away!" ■

"Although their total build costs came well within their predicted budget of £50–55,000, the couple also warn against setting too tight a budget."

Useful Contacts

Designer – David Lloyd: 02380 693741

Bricks – Michelmersh Brick and Tile Co: 01794 368506

Reclaimed ridge tiles – Romsey Reclamation: 01794 524174

Windows – Abbot Joinery: 01825 872567

Front door — Magnet: 01535 661133

Roof Slates – Embee TS (Blunn Slates Ltd): 01703 331775

Kitchen – MFI: Local branches

Range Cooker – Belling Farmhouse: 01709 579900

Rooflight – Velux: 01592 772211

Boiler – Glow-Worm: 01773 824141

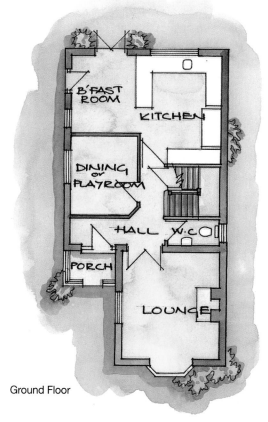

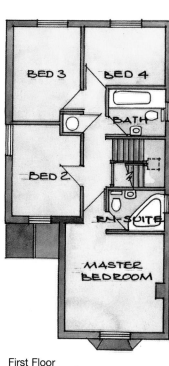

Ground Floor

First Floor

Character Building

Hadyn and Wendy Wood have adapted a standard timber frame kit house to create a new home that has all of the character of a traditional cottage.

Words:
Clive Fewins

Photography:
Nigel Rigden

Walking past the cottage home of Haydn and Wendy Wood in a leafy Berkshire lane, with its timbered exterior, rendered gable ends, mature roof of rugged handmade clay tiles, neat dormer windows and attractive herringbone brick infill panels, it is easy to conclude that it has stood there for several hundred years. The reality is that they moved in during the spring of 2000 and that even when the house was two thirds complete the deception was so good that the team sent by Potton, their timber frame suppliers, to undertake the second fix woodwork drove up and down the road trying to find it. Small wonder then that the house was declared outright winner of the Potton Self-Build Awards 2002.

For Haydn and Wendy it all started seven years ago, when they were keen to move from their three-bedroomed mid terrace house on an estate in Wokingham to a historic cottage, preferably not too far away. When they realised that the sort of historic cottage they were looking for was beyond their pockets they decided to self-build. Armed with all the magazines they could muster they scoured land agencies, got hold of a local plan and maps and consulted friends over a wide area. Then one day Haydn spotted an unkempt area of garden behind a hedge that appeared to belong to a large private house in a village on the outskirts of Reading.

"It was about a fifth of an acre and very overgrown, except for a lawn at the front – quite large enough to take a house of the size we wanted plus a reasonable-sized garden," says Haydn, who runs a live music management company.

When he knocked on the door of the house Haydn was told the land actually belonged to a developer who had owned it for several years but permitted them to use it as an extension to their garden. Haydn and Wendy made contact with the developer, who agreed to sell them the plot for £100,000. Before purchasing they approached their local council for planning consent. It turned out to be a battle royale.

"Despite the fact that we proposed a relatively modest infill in a vernacular style there were 78 letters of objection from local people, including the parish council and the local amenity society," Haydn says. "The whole process, including the public appeal which we finally won with the assistance of a planning consultant, took 12 months."

By the time the purchase was complete Haydn and Wendy had fallen in love with the 137m² Caxton model in the Potton timber framed range. They wished to reverse the layout downstairs, placing the lounge on the left hand side facing the front and the kitchen and dining room to the right of the hallway. This would give them a larger lounge than had it been the other way round. It also meant they were able to extend the lounge to give a sunroom at the south-east of the rear of the house.

"It was a perfect arrangement for all our entertaining and also meant that we could take advantage of the morning sun," says Wendy. "Potton proved very amenable to all this and several other changes – in fact most adaptable," says Haydn. "They were also happy to add a porch at the front, which added greatly to the traditional cottage look we wanted to achieve. By using Potton to do the redesign in this way and erect the shell and the roof structure, it gave us confidence. As novice self-builders we had the security of knowing that we were supported by a major timber frame company with a lot of experience of self-build and whom we could talk to on a daily basis if we so desired."

Haydn and ▶ Wendy came across 30 leaded windows they fell in love with; Potton redesigned the window openings to fit.

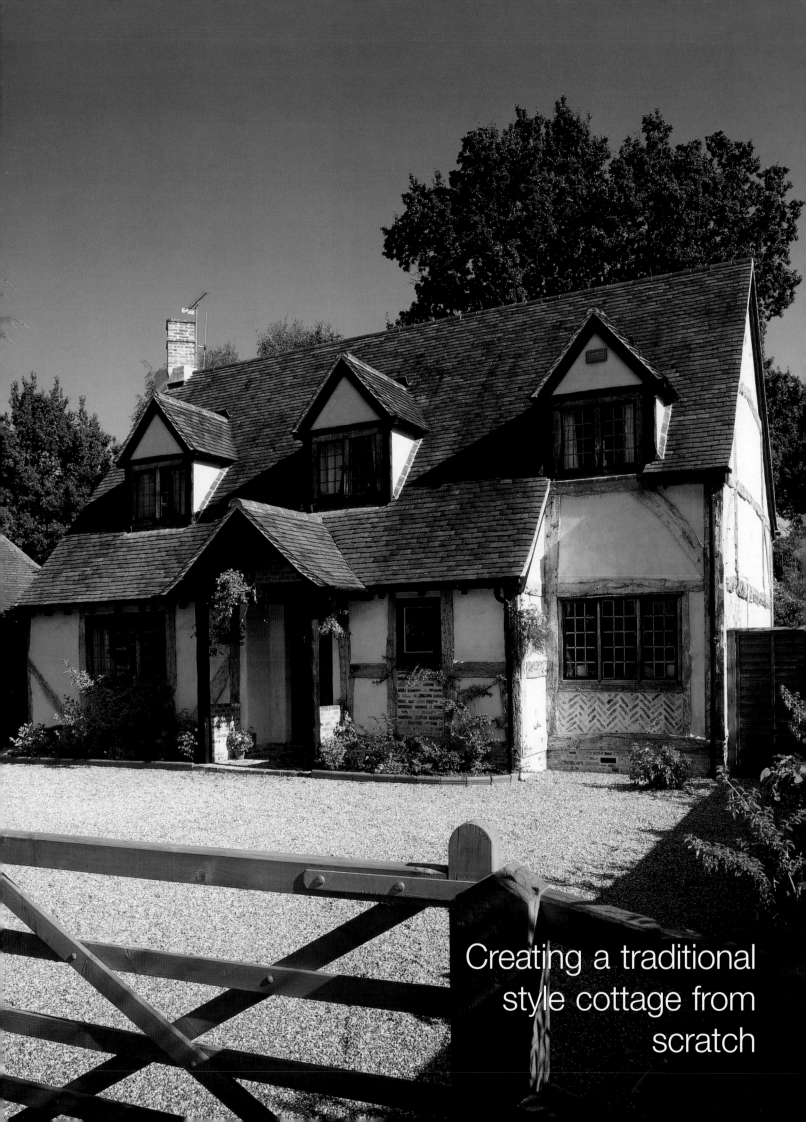

Creating a traditional
style cottage from
scratch

During the lengthy planning stage Haydn and Wendy worked hard at sourcing all the reclaimed materials they thought they would need in order to achieve their aim of making the new cottage look more like a renovation. They managed to obtain reclaimed handmade clay rooftiles, genuinely old oak timbers, and 'Elizabethan-style' two inch bricks, some of them several hundred years old, for a few of the exterior wall panels.

In the course of this hunt they had an extraordinary find. One of the demolition contractors they got to know informed them of a 14 bedroomed, early 20th century house in Maidenhead that was due to come down to make way for a small housing estate.

"We went there to look at oak flooring but ended up buying 30 oak square leaded light windows and doors at £100 each," says Haydn. "We selected the ones we could use and sold the rest for £3,000, so all our lovely high quality oak windows cost us nothing!" By the time they

"Really we built the house to suit the windows. The Potton designers resized every window opening."

had some broken panes repaired and a double door made to enter the sun room they were £2,000 worse off – but it still proved a pretty good deal.

Once on site in May 1999 the first task was to move a 35ft tall cedar tree which had a preservation order on it. It now stands happily near the front entrance. After this, putting down the beam and block foundations and erecting the timber frame proved straightforward.

"We scoured reclamation yards from Cornwall to Cambridge for materials," Haydn says. "All the old beams came from Antique Buildings of Dunsfold in Sussex where owner Peter Barker had some 300 year-old oak sawn as planks that he usually sold as cladding. They proved perfect for the idea I had in mind, which was to adapt the Potton ▶

▲ **Haydn sourced the old beams from Antique Buildings (01428 609444).**

method – using planks of stained or painted Douglas Fir to give a mock Tudor appearance – and make it look much more authentic by using planks of genuine reclaimed oak fixed to lightweight insulated blockwork and surrounded by a lime render."

The deception of the exterior timbers is totally effective, partly because of the depth of the rugged lime render but also because of ingenious methods of masking the deception, mainly devised by Haydn.

"Really we built the outer walls of the house twice to achieve the effect we wanted…"

The blockwork is separated from the Potton timber frame by a clear cavity. Together with the insulation in the blocks this has given the house added insulation values, which has meant that they have been able to do away with the requirement for double glazing.

"We were very careful to check with our extremely helpful building control officer that the insulation values in the roof and walls and floors would counteract the windows, which are not thermally efficient, before we bought them," says Haydn. "Fortunately he appreciated the exceptional quality of the windows and approved. This was a great bonus for us as the windows were a great find and we were adamant that we did not want double glazing.

"With the old glass and the warped leadwork in many of the lights the light catches every single pane in a delightful way and the effect is one of a myriad of reflections. Really we built the house to suit the windows. The Potton designers resized every window opening in the house to take them, which was fantastic. They also did some very clever manipulation so we could have our new ▶

The traditional ▶ style kitchen was from Top Door (01206 796692).

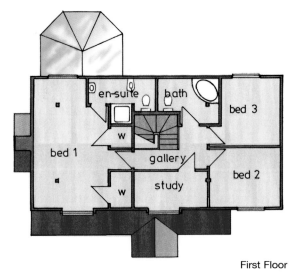

First Floor

FLOORPLAN: Hadyn and Wendy reconfigured the upstairs of Potton's standard plan to give them a larger master bedroom with a vaulted ceiling and en suite bathroom.

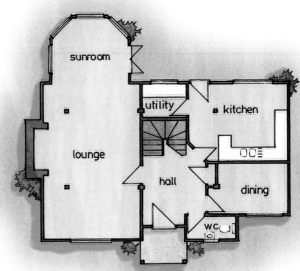

Ground Floor

Fact File costs as of March 2003

NAMES: Haydn and Wend Wood

PROFESSIONS: Live music promoter and freelance trainer

AREA: Berkshire

HOUSE TYPE: Four bedroom detached

HOUSE SIZE: 150m²

BUILD ROUTE: Selves as main contractor

CONSTRUCTION: Timber frame with exterior blockwork skin

WARRANTY: Zurich

FINANCE: Private + mortgage

BUILD TIME: May 1999 – May 2000

LAND COST: £100,000

BUILD COST: £132,500

TOTAL COST: £232,500

HOUSE VALUE: £600,000

COST/m²: £883

68% COST SAVING

Cost Breakdown:

Professional fees £6,300
Groundwork & foundations . .£7,700
Connections £3,400

First fix carpentry + other labour . . .
. . . .£1,800
Scaffold and other hire £3,500
Timber frame £29,500
Roof tiles + fittings £7,600
Roof labour £2,500
Bricks, blocks + Anki chimney £5,700
Labour – brick + block £4,600
UFH + central ventilation system . . .
. . . .£5,100
Bathroom + plumbing fittings £6,100
Plumbing; labour £3,100
Electrical fittings + security . .£3,700
Electrics; labour £2,200
Built in vac system £500
Doors, windows + glazing . . .£3,800
Oak front door £2,200
Plastering + screeding £3,100
External finishes £4,500
Kitchen £6,000
Second fix carpentry £4,600
Hard floors £2,600
Floorboards £500
Insulation materials £1,700
Other labour £5,800
Other building supplies . . .£10,900
– VAT reclaim . . . .-£6,500

TOTAL £132,500

bespoke solid oak front door, which we obtained from a company in Yorkshire.

"Really we built the outer walls of the house twice to achieve the effect we wanted," Wendy says. "We don't regret the added expense of doing this because the result is everything we always wanted it to be. The plot was expensive – several years ago building land was changing hands at £1m an acre round here – but the building costs came out quite reasonable as we sub-contracted and did a huge amount of work ourselves. For a total outlay of £232,500 we now have a four bedroomed house of great character that is worth well in excess of £600,000." ■

USEFUL CONTACTS: **Design** – Selves plus Potton: 01480 401401; **Timber Frame** – Potton: 01480 401401; **Planning consultant/Engineer** – Robin Bradbeer: 01453 889102; **Tree mover** – Ruskins: 01277 810101; **Carpentry first fix** – Timber construction: 01462 674481; **Second fix** – MJD: 0118 978 8908; **Groundworks** – Chris James: 0118 934 0001; **Bricklayer** – Joe Duffy: 0118 969 4698; **Electrician** – Alan Abbott: 01276 32479; **Plumbing** – Arthur Reid: 07770 437543; **Leadwork and glazing** – Leadcraft: 0118 956 8534; **Patio doors** – Lattice Windows: 01386 701079; **Lime mortar** – IJP: 0118 969 6949; **Roofing contractor** – Trevor Chamberlain: 0118 930 3433; **Plastering/renders** – Eamonn O'Conner: 0118 961 8636; **Underfloor heating** – Nu-Heat: 01404 549770; **Ventilation and heat recovery** – Villavent: 01993 778481; **Kitchen** – Top Door: 01206 796692; **Oak front door** – Heritage Oak: 01422 348231; **Reclaimed sawn oak posts and beams** – Drummonds: 01428 609444; **Rooftiles** – Giles of Stokenchurch: 01494 482396; **S&T Roofing**: 020 8684 2801; **Limestone flooring** – Artisan: 01380 720007; **Terracotta flooring** – Terracotta Direct: 01284 3880022; **Historic bricks** – Drummonds: 01428 609444; **Cast iron guttering** – Sinclair: 01952 262500

DIY Landscaping

Taking on the daunting task of resurrecting the abandoned land surrounding their home saved Robert and Lulie Hunt a fortune and gave them a great sense of achievement. We ask how, and why, they did it.

When Robert & Lulie Hunt first clapped eyes on their Herefordshire home, it was a two up two down cottage that had been left empty for some time. The gardens were overgrown and the hedges were wild but they could see the potential and were looking for something to "really have a go at."

Now, five years later, that neglected cottage has been transformed into a four bedroom home, set in its own landscaped grounds, with the most stunning views down to the Wye valley. They've undertaken most of the work themselves, working as a team but we wanted to discuss their experiences of recovering and landscaping the extensive grounds and gardens.

What was it like when you first came?

A total wilderness. It had been unoccupied for about 18 months and the whole garden was overrun with brambles, nettles and weeds. Nevertheless, it was the garden that drew us to the place – that and the greenhouse. Even now, after all we've done to the house, it's the outside that's important to us. We could walk through the bottom of the hedges but couldn't see over the top. When they were clipped, we found that we'd gained ground and uncovered great views.

Hidden in the undergrowth were the shapes of flowerbeds full of buttercups and thistles. They were hell to get rid of. All we could do was dig and dig but underneath were these old fashioned pelargoniums and herbaceous border shrubs. The top section had been planted with Christmas trees. We cut all those down and winched the roots out by anchoring to the oak tree by the garage. When the undergrowth was removed and the stump ground up for mulch, we were able to think about terracing the bank and putting in steps. The first few months were all just chopping and burning.

And the lawns? From the early photographs they look irredeemable.

We thought so at first but in fact, once we'd cut down the huge growth, we managed to get them back. We sieved soil into the holes and just mowed and rolled it. It's taken three years but that's the original grass.

We've created new flowerbeds – our Ying and Yang beds. I prefer shrubs to annuals and in the banks and the rockery, I prefer native wild flowers. Recovering old flowerbeds is a voyage of discovery – a trip back in time.

Yet it's not just soft but hard landscaping that you've done.

That's true – Robert got a cement mixer for Christmas. I'd never laid stone before. It was, of course, all in the ground here and when we excavated the bank we had as much as we needed for all of the steps, retaining walls and the rockery. We got a quote for the stonework but it was horrendous. An old chap came and showed me how to do it and I had a go. It was great – physically demanding but so relaxing. At the end of the day when you brush it down and stand back, it's such a satisfying feeling.

The steps up the bank are made from railway sleepers costing £10 each, with gravel as the steps and the curved walling in stone. We got the idea from the planked steps in the forest and just scaled it up.

The only other hard landscaping is the Cotswold gravel driveway and the patio areas. We went for the 20mm instead of pea shingle as it doesn't migrate in the tyres. Rather than going for total coverage in the patio area we've opted for slabs set within the gravel and then merged that into the pathway areas.

The crowning glory, apart from the flowerbeds and lawns, is undoubtedly the conservatory.

That's really what we bought the house for. Everything else was immaterial. I don't know what it's made of, maybe shuttered and poured concrete, maybe brick and roughcast. If so, I don't know how they got these shapes and arches. We've restored it as we found it, retaining the metal framed windows and roof. And, of course, the vines. One red and one white growing in from the outside. We've not had a vintage year yet but it's coming.

So has the work gone out of the garden now?

No, with a garden like this you're never really finished and it's almost a full time job. But the major bits are done and now it's just a question of maintenance. What we've done will gently mature. That's if the badgers and wild boar stop trying to dig it all up! ∎

"The quote for building the steps, retaining walls and rockery was horrendous…doing it myself was physically demanding, but so relaxing…"

Frederick East has built a comfortable new bungalow with garage below on a remarkably low budget.

Words:
David Snell

Photography:
Nicholas Toyne

When Frederick East had the first opportunity to show his wife Audrey the new bungalow he had built for them, she had only one word to say – "Brilliant!" She was referring to the finished home of course, although many would attribute that epithet to Frederick himself and the fact that, in his mid 70s, he had not only devised, drawn and planned the whole project, but he'd gone on to build it himself.

In 1989 Frederick and Audrey returned to this country after living for several years in San Diego and bought a Bovis home at the head of a small cul-de-sac development overlooking Exeter. It was a peaceful spot that, in the end, neither of them wanted to move away from. Nevertheless, in 1997, after Audrey had experienced a bout of illness, they both decided that they really needed to downsize to a smaller property. "I noticed that our house was on a considerably larger plot than all of the other houses," says Frederick, "and I decided to go down to the council and see if we could develop part of our garden."

There was sufficient room for a new house, but with a slope of 3m front to back, the original developers, Bovis, had obviously decided that it was not worth developing, as it would need a one off design. Frederick, however, made use of the slope, designing a bungalow with a basement garage beneath, partially built into the slope. He set about doing all of his own drawings, including detailed electrical and plumbing layouts, and then made successful planning and Building Regulations applications.

Work commenced in September 1997 and Frederick had by this stage decided that he was going to source all of the materials himself and use labour-only subcontractors. It was a quiet time for building in the southwest – consequently labour was plentiful and there were some good deals to be had on materials. "It always amazes me just how cheap things are in bulk," Frederick maintains.

Local builders – a two man gang with an occasional third made up by the leader's father – were contracted to do all of the groundwork and to build the superstructure up to roof plate, including the first/ground floor joists. 460 tonnes of spoil had to be sent away and the foundations were soon in, ready for the below ground blockwork that, in places, was 1.2m thick, tanked and waterproofed for the garage. Frederick loved watching the gang work. The old ▶

"I wanted to ▶ get all the living accommodation on one level," Frederick explains, "and that meant that, with windows to habitable rooms on both sides, the overall width of the building was fairly limited."

BUILT FOR £32,000

Designing and building your own home

"I don't want to be a smarty but it does seem to me to come down to common sense," says Frederick. "I have always been practical with my hands and really this was terrific fun."

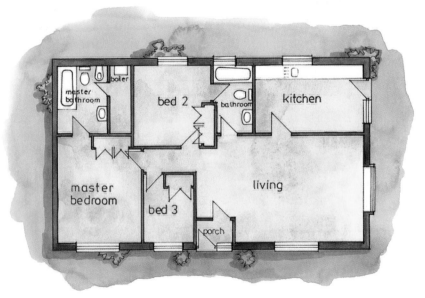

man would mix up the mortar, his son would apply it to the bed and then the youngest of them would pick up the block and place it so that the builder could tap into place, level, and butter up the end.

A Cornish timber company quoted to supply and fix the roof, which they did in a day and then Frederick hired two subcontractors to felt, batten and tile the roof. "That was the important point," he recalls. "When we had a weather-tight shell up, I could relax to some extent and do the rest at my leisure whilst having the luxury of living next door."

Over the next few months Frederick, working on his own, laid the decking, put up the studwork partitioning,

"I had wanted to have warm air central heating. It works so well in the USA…"

carcassed the plumbing and electrics and got things ready for the dry liners. Whilst living in the USA he had been impressed with fibreboard and, not knowing that a similar product was readily available in the UK, arranged to have a complete pallet shipped over for use on all the walls and ceilings. That was about the only innovation he borrowed from his time abroad. "I had wanted to have warm air central heating. It works so well in the USA," he insists, "but all the advice I got here was that I would never be able to sell it. So in the end I stuck with radiators."

Frederick did all of the second fix plumbing, electrics and carpentry, shopping around for bargains to such a degree that two complete bathroom suites cost just £550. He laid the ceramic tiled floors, tiled the walls and did the base coat decoration before handing over to a decorator to finish off. Frederick's work was not done, however – outside, he single handedly took on the task of hand-digging all of the drainage trenches down the side of the bungalow, constructing the sloping approach ramps – "In case I need them when I'm old" – and all of the retaining brickwork.

The bungalow was finished in May 1998 but it took a full year to find a buyer for the old house and in the meantime, sadly, Audrey became ill again and was diagnosed with breast cancer and had to enter a hospice.

In June 1999 she moved into her new finished home for the first time and made her one word pronouncement. She died at home three months later, inordinately proud of her husband's achievements, and thrilled with her wonderful new home. ■

Fact File costs as of July 2002

NAMES: Frederick and Audrey East

PROFESSIONS: Retired

AREA: Exeter

HOUSE TYPE: 3 bedroom bungalow with garage under

HOUSE SIZE: 90m²

BUILD ROUTE: Self managed plus own labour

CONSTRUCTION: Blockwork rendered with brick detail

WARRANTY: NHBC 'Solo'

SAP RATING: 82

FINANCE: Private

BUILD TIME: Sept '97 – May '98

LAND COST: Nil (EST £22,000)

BUILD COST: £32,360		**69%**
TOTAL COST: £54,360		**COST**
HOUSE VALUE: £175,000		**SAVING**
COST/m²: £360		

Cost Breakdown:

Shell builders inc render	£8,000
Soil away	£2,100
Supply and fix roof	£1,800
Roof tilers	£650
Fibreboard	£700
Dry liners	£730
Finishing decorator	£200
Sanitaryware	£500
Other labour & services	£2,000
Materials	£15,680
TOTAL	**£32,360**

Useful Contacts

Boiler – Halstead Boilers:	01787 475557
Rooftiles – Redland Roofing Systems:	01306 872000
Fibreboard manufacturers – Fels (UK) Ltd.:	0121 321 1155

DIY House Design

Fed up with paying over the odds for architects to work on designs that he'd come up with himself, Malcolm Cadwallader decided to use CAD packages to create his own drawings. We find out how he got on.

In 1992 Malcolm Cadwallader started his own business. When it got going sufficiently well for him to let go of the reins, he and wife Clare started to look around for a plot of land for a self-build project.

They sold their home and bought a smaller house, releasing £80,000 in equity, then spent 18 months searching for land before they finally bought a plot at auction.

It was a semi detached bungalow requiring demolition and the careful conversion of the remaining party wall into an end gable. There were restrictive covenants that needed an indemnity policy, a rising sewage main that required access and it was a sloping site.

When we spoke to them they'd just started work on their own new home and were up to first lift. They're building a split level 3-4 bedroom dwelling that's estimated to be worth £240,000. What we wanted to talk to them about was their experience in doing all of their own drawings and handling their own Planning and Building Regulations applications.

What made you take the unusual step of not using an architect?

We were going to, even though we'd had horrendous previous experiences. We went and saw some architects but they always seemed to want to go in a different direction to the one we wanted to go. We got a quote of £4,000 for just the Planning & Building Regs and £10,000 for the full service and decided that we just didn't want to spend that money. Plus the fact that we realised that the only way we were going to get what we wanted was to draw it out ourselves in the first place. We questioned why we should be paying somebody £4,000 to do a minimal amount of work to our own designs — it was like throwing money down the drain. Then a friend of a friend gave us the software package AutoCad and we began to get stuck in.

Presumably you were computer literate and capable of working it?

Not a bit of it. It was impossible — I couldn't do a thing with it! Then a friend came and showed me, I went through the tutorials and my son bought me a book on it. It would have taken years to master but I sat at it every day for a month. I was determined it wasn't going to beat me!

Then it just clicked and suddenly I could do it. I don't know it all, it might do loads more than I know as there are so many options and it's ten times worse than Excel or Word. Still, I managed to be able to produce drawings. We'd sketched them out beforehand then fed in the details and there they were. The results were instantaneous. It's great because you're drawing full scale and you can move around in the machine and view it from different angles in 2D. It also has 3D but let's be realistic!

We read the planning guidelines and visited the planner with the first drafts. He said they were the best drawings he'd seen and we pretty soon got to the point where we made the submission with 20 A4 CAD drawings – nothing by pen and ruler.

So the planning sailed through?

Not exactly. The staff changed and the new girl had a totally different point of view. She didn't like our proposals at all and really gave me the impression that she resented having to deal with us direct rather than through an agent. We had to change the garage from one side to the other, which in hindsight is a good thing, even though it cost us more on foundations. She wanted a street scene view, so I did it on the AutoCad with the levels I'd taken on site — I

▲ Despite being almost totally inexperienced with computers, Malcolm picked up the architectural design package quite easily. Using the drawings designed on the package, he applied for and achieved planning approval, saving £1,000s in architect's fees.

was surprised when she accepted it. She hated the fact that we were making up the land at the front to mitigate the slope on the drive and argued about the relative ridge heights. Eventually she suggested we go back to square one and start again. I dug in — I replied to her assertions and queries one by one and we contacted our local councillor, who was also the chair of the planning committee. The next thing we heard was that she'd recommended approval. It had taken seven months.

And has the building gone according to the, er, plans?

It has so far, except for a couple of minor alterations on the drains. I wouldn't want the readers to run away with the idea that everybody should do it. It's fraught with pitfalls and we still don't know that we're home and dry yet, although happily it looks that way. You've got to have the time to be able to read everything and tie it all together, so that in satisfying one regulation you're not compromising another. ■

"We questioned why we should be paying somebody £4,000 to do a minimal amount of work to our own designs."

Words: **Michael Holmes**

Photography: **Nigel Rigden**

The Phillips' home is loosely based on the design of a traditional Suffolk barn. The exterior is clad in pressure treated feather edged softwood and the tiles are Old English Antique from Sandtoft.

Affordable Luxury

DIY self-builders Keith and Cynthia Phillips have managed to build a spacious, high quality house for a fraction of what the property is now worth.

A budget of £84,000 does not buy a lot of house in East Anglia these days, unless, that is, you are prepared to build it yourself. This is exactly what Keith and Cynthia Phillips realised when they decided to fulfil a longstanding ambition and build their own home. "Given that I am already semi-retired and that Cynthia retires in three years time, we did not want to have a mortgage," says Keith. "Our budget for a new home, therefore, was what we had left over from the sale of our house, around £84,000, and we were determined to stick to this. Self-building meant better value for money."

Most people who try to build a large house on a modest budget manage to do so only by compromising on quality and whilst no one likes to admit it, this usually shows in the end result. Far from cutting corners, however, Keith and Cynthia, whose new home is loosely based on the style of a traditional timber barn, have managed to stretch their £84,000 further than seems possible, allowing them to build to a very high specification. The interiors are finished with an abundance of high quality timber and they even managed to find funds to install luxury features such as a central vacuum system and whole house ventilation with heat recovery. And whilst most budget new homes are very basic in their design, the Phillips' 205m² property includes some impressive design features, most notably a dramatic double height hallway with a galleried 'bridge' landing overlooking a feature window that stretches from floor to roof.

Whilst they may not have had much money to work with, what the Phillips did have on their side was time. Their main tactic to keep down costs, therefore, was to use subcontract labour only where essential.

▶

▲ The low cost per square metre was partly achieved because the design makes maximum use of available space, including attic bedrooms.

The kitchen ▶ cost just £850 from MFI. The suspended ceiling allows access to all services.

"I hired a groundworker with a JCB digger to clear the site," says Keith. "We also used him to divert a mains sewer that ran right across the middle of the plot and to dig the trenches. I then took over from there, getting in help only to move and position heavy items such as the concrete beams for the ground floor slab and to position the roof trusses.

"We chose to build using blockwork because I could do this all myself," explains Keith. "I would have liked to build with a timber frame, but this would have had to be made in a factory and so there would have been additional labour costs. It was a compromise, but it was necessary."

One thing Keith was not prepared to compromise on, however, was fuel economy, choosing to insulate the blockwork walls to a standard far superior to that required by the building regulations. "I used two layers of blockwork with mineral wool batts in the cavity, and a further 25mm layer of Celotex urethane insulation behind the timber cladding on the outside," he explains.

The structural shell of the house was weathertight within a year and Keith began working on the internal trades during the spring of 2000. Whilst he was happy to take on the first fix plumbing himself, using OSMA Gold plastic pipe and fittings which are ideal for the DIYer, he opted to leave the electrics to a subcontractor. He then dry lined the house by himself, fixing the plasterboard on dabs with the joints taped and filled – a skill that is easier to master than wet plastering and which requires less drying out time. The electrician was then brought back in to complete the second fix whilst Keith took on the rest of the finishing trades himself with the exception of the staircase, which was supplied and fitted by a local joiner. ▶

The double height hallway, with bridge landing and barn door style window openings, is a remarkable feature for a house costing just £225/m².

The parish council objected to the design, but the Phillips stood their ground and with the officers on their side, won the day.

Ground Floor

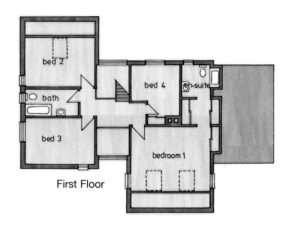

First Floor

After decorating and landscaping, the final build cost was a remarkably low £225/m².

"Part of the economy is in making maximum use of available space," says Keith. "I also had to battle with the planners over the choice of rooftiles. They wanted us to use handmade clay pantiles at over twice the price of the machine made clay pantiles that we used from Sandtoft."

Keith also stood his ground with suppliers, always researching the best prices for all of the materials and never afraid to return substandard items. "We found that Travis Perkins offered us the best prices on timber and joinery, whilst for kitchens, bathrooms and lighting we used places like MFI and B&Q," says Cynthia.

"We feel we have developed quite a talent for achieving a quality finish on a shoestring," adds Keith. "For example, in the three bathrooms we wanted fitted vanity units, but

they would have been way over our budget allowance. We achieved a comparable result at a third of the price by adapting kitchen wall units."

Although the couple knew exactly the accommodation they wanted, they hired a local architect to draw up their plans and to handle their planning and building regulations applications.

"We made a few mistakes," admits Keith. "We should have put the boiler in the garage rather than the utility room to save space, and we should have positioned the lounge differently in order to take advantage of the views over fields to the back of the property, but these are all small in the scheme of things.

"We are proud to have achieved such an individual and highly specified house on a total budget of £84,000. We would have been unable to afford a comparable property any other way." ∎

Fact File costs as of Jan 2003

NAMES: Keith and Cynthia Phillips

PROFESSIONS: Retired Handyman and Social Worker

AREA: Suffolk

HOUSE TYPE: Two bedroom detached

HOUSE SIZE: 184m² plus 21m² integral garage

BUILD ROUTE: DIY plus subcontractors

CONSTRUCTION: Blockwork cavity walls with timber cladding

WARRANTY: None

SAP RATING: Not known

FINANCE: Private

BUILD TIME: June 1999 – Dec 2000

LAND COST: £38,000

BUILD COST: £46,000	**72%**
TOTAL COST: £84,000	**COST**
CURRENT VALUE: £300,000	**SAVING**
COST/m²: £225	

Cost Breakdown:

Professional Fees	.£2,000
Groundworks	.£2,600
Structural Shell to 2nd Fix	.£18,080
Services	.£1,300
Plumbing & Heating	.£2,700
Electrics	.£1,800
Kitchen, Utility & Bathrooms	.£4,200
Joinery	.£6,140
Cent. Vacuum & Heat Recovery	£1,600
Decorating	.£700
Landscaping	.£1,380
Miscellaneous	.£3,500
TOTAL	.£46,000

USEFUL CONTACTS: **Architect** - John Putman: 01986 892454; **Ceramic Tiles** - Topps Tiles: 0800 138 1671; **Roof Tiles** - Sandtoft (Old English Antique pantiles): 01427 871200; **Timber** - Travis Perkins: 01604 752424; **Kitchen** - MFI: 0870 6075093; **Plastic Plumbing** - OSMA Gold: 01249 766600; **Central Vacuum System** - Available from Total Home: 01386 849000; **Whole House Ventilation** - Hampton: 01635 569933; **Doors and Windows** - John Carr (Jeld-Wen): 0870 1260000; **Staircase and feature windows** - Andrew Bale: 01508 518667; **Insulation** - Celotex: 01473 820888 **Staircase & Feature Windows – John Bale:** 01508 518667; **Electrician** - John Lewis 01986 781303

DIY Decorating

Self-builder Sally Andrews and her mother Joyce discovered that decorating is not just a matter of putting on paint. Undeterred by the hard work, Sally even went on to create a trompe l'oeil.

▲ **A Trompe l'Oeil is a painting designed to give the illusion of reality.**

"So many people tried their very best to dissuade us from building our new bungalow," remembers Sally Andrews. "But I insisted on it," says Joyce, her mother. "It was something I'd always wanted to do and the fact that I was approaching 80 seemed no reason not to."

About five years ago some alarming cracks appeared in their pre-fabricated concrete bungalow near Cheltenham and the porch section started to detach itself. Far from seeing this as a disaster, however, Joyce was determined that she was going to take the opportunity of fulfilling a long held dream.

"As much as I loved the old bungalow, I'd always really wanted a proper brick built home and I saw this as my chance." Sally and Joyce had limited funds as the insurance payout on the bungalow was paltry, so they decided to build by managing the subcontractors themselves and using their own expertise in the form of decoration and final finishes. The consequent saving on labour costs amounted to around £2,000.

At what point did you realise what you'd taken on with the decoration?

We had decided that we would not be that good at clambering around on scaffolding and, in any event, time becomes so important on a building project that we really did not want to hold up the other trades and, most importantly, delay the completion. So we actually got a painter and decorator to do the fascias and soffits as well as the Sadolin coats to the external windows and all we really took on was the internal decoration. That is when we discovered that decoration is not just a matter of painting things and that preparation is the

major part of the trade. We sanded down and filed all of the doors, skirtings and architraves before knotting and priming them. The timber was surprisingly rough but we had a very good plasterer and although there were a few patches, in general we did not have to bother with the walls.

Decoration is often thought of as easy but it really is an art and in fact the decorator is responsible for making good all of the other trades. You can be as careful as you like with the topcoat gloss finish but if you are not putting it on a well prepared and smooth surface you might as well not bother.

Did the pastel colouring you've gone for influence the trompe l'oeil?

No, that really happened by accident. The first intention was to have a display alcove with shelves for all my plates. We had it built and the lighting put over the top of the arch. Finished, but without the shelves, it seemed so empty and I suddenly thought that it was exactly the right place for a trompe l'oeil. I got a picture off an old plate we had with a sort of dreamy Grecian scene. I drew it out as big as I could on paper and marked it up into squares. Then I scaled it up to where it was going to go and marked the grid on the wall so that I could get all of the sections right. I had to change some of the detail, as pictures often lose their proportions when they are enlarged. It is important not to be too fussy and to think out your designs carefully.

"It is also important to position it properly and not to allow it to dominate the room. Do you want to view it from a normal sitting position or as you enter the room? Your eye is deceived – that is what these paintings are supposed to do

– so it is essential that you get the horizon right, or it does not work. An effective trick is to allow the painting to 'spill over' into the room by the addition of something like an ivy trail that creeps out from the frame.

As well as fixing the tiling you also decorated the tiles yourselves?

Yes, I have done trompe l'oeil for other people in the area but the thing I really like doing is the tiles. I bought plain tiles and decorated them for the kitchen and the bathrooms. You need to choose tile colours that will accept a design and allow their background colouring to form the lighter sections. I find that those by Pilkington are best as they retain their glazed surface when re-fired.

Obviously it is something that you need a kiln in order to do, although not a high temperature one. You have to start off with the pattern or painting and transpose that to the tiles using graphite paper or a pencil. Then you begin to build up your colours, starting with the lighter ones and gradually building up the shadow and detail of the bolder shades. It can mean repeating the firing process up to four or five times to get it just how you want and to get the depth of colour. ∎

"Decoration is not just a matter of painting things… preparation is the major part of the trade."

Phil and Caroline Pearson have built a spacious, individually designed, family home on a total budget of £90,000.

Words:
David Snell

Photography:
Geoff Harris

One of the ▶ ways in which Phil and Caroline kept costs down was by doing a lot of work themselves. Phil fitted the kitchen himself, with a little help from the builder.

Unlike many self-builders, Phil and Caroline Pearson harboured no great ambition to build their own home. They had heard of other people building but had never seriously considered the idea themselves. They were happy where they were and in any event, they would never be able to find a decent plot – or so they thought. "Little did we realise," Phil remembers, "that the plot was right under our noses the whole time."

The Pearsons lived in one of a row of semi-detached houses, most of which had fairly reasonable back gardens about 8 metres wide by about 54 metres deep. Except, that is, for Phil and Caroline's. Theirs extended for 92 metres, well beyond all of the others, in a long strip of land that went between all of the gardens of the houses backing onto theirs, right through to the road at the rear. "We didn't really use it," says Phil, "and to be honest, it was a bit of a jungle back there."

Then one day, Phil was out in the garden talking to his neighbour over the fence. "He was complaining about having to mow his lawn and he asked me if I would be interested in buying half his garden and incorporating it into mine – perhaps to build a house on," recalls Phil.

"I carried on gardening for a bit but what he'd said was churning around in my mind, so I called across to him and asked him whether he was serious. He said that he was and so I asked him what he wanted for it, suggesting figures from £1,000 right up to £10,000. We eventually settled on £5,000, subject to getting planning permission." ▶

Built

for £85,000

An individual home on a budget

▲ The 'family room' on the plans has become a formal dining room, with glazed doors to keep light flowing through.

Back indoors, Phil told Caroline all about the conversation and she was as surprised as he was at this strange turn of events. Gradually, the two of them got used to the idea and the more they thought about the potential, the keener they got.

The next thing was to consult the planners to see if it was possible. They said that they had no objections in principle, so long as the semi-detached houses were left with reasonable back gardens. But, as Phil explains, "if we left the old houses with back gardens about 24 metres deep we still ended up with a plot that was over 17 metres wide by about 30 metres deep. Plus, of course, the strip of land that would form our access onto the road."

Lopping the back gardens off the existing houses wouldn't affect their value to any great degree because, in reality, their gardens were, as the neighbour had realised, too long anyway. But there was always the chance that other neighbours would object, either in principle or on the grounds of overlooking, so Phil and Caroline started to do as much research as they could in order to be able to counteract any argument.

"We decided that we just had to bite the bullet and that we really had to give this opportunity a go," Caroline remembers. "So we took our original sketch ideas to a local house designer and he turned them into workable plans and applied for full planning permission," Phil interjects. "He favoured timber frame construction and he

put us onto Guardian Homes who gave us a price for the manufacture and supply of the frame, plus its erection.

Phil continues: "I'd already decided that, due to work commitments, I didn't want to have too much to do with the actual construction process and that, if we could, we'd build on more or less a turnkey basis. But when all the prices came in they were way too high and we had to come to terms with the fact that, if we were going to get this thing done, we'd have to project manage it ourselves."

Phil is a maintenance engineer for British Gas but he had never done any building before and although he knew a little of the build process, this was breaking new ground. "I found it quite enjoyable and I managed to formulate a programme against which I could put prices to the various trades and components. I was quite proud of it, although when I showed it to John Coward of Coward & Kerr, the builders we eventually used, I fully expected him to laugh. He didn't, which was quite pleasing, but he did say that we wouldn't meet all of our targets, especially the time schedule. Nevertheless, it was a good starting point. If the sequences are right then, after that, it is really only blocks of time that overlap each other to one degree or another."

Whilst all of this preliminary work was going on, the planning application was running into a little bit of trouble following objections from some of the neighbours and the planner's own queries about the degree of overlooking. Phil borrowed a level and by careful calculations was able to prove that the lie of the land meant that the new house wouldn't be intrusive. It meant that the application took a little longer but they did eventually get approval, allowing them to complete the purchase of the land from their neighbour.

Work started on site in February 2000. "Caroline and I had got used to the fact that we were going to have to be

involved in the management of our project and that we were going to employ professionals for the main trades," Phil recalls. "Nevertheless, I was going to help out with some of the easier tasks."

Builder, John Coward, brought the house up to oversite after which Guardian Homes came in and erected the timber frame. There then followed a bit of a hold up. "Some of the PVC-u items such as the windows, doors and walk in bays didn't turn up on time and that meant that the roofers couldn't start until nearly three weeks later," recalls Phil. "But they had the roof felted and battened in just three days and the tiling finished completely three days after that. In just two months from starting we had a weathertight shell, our house was there and we could start work inside whilst the builders got on with the external works and the face brickwork."

With the house in the dry, the second fix tradesmen moved in, with Phil helping out. "I bought the stuff for the electrician and he told me how and where to run the

"Just two months from starting we had a weathertight shell, our house was there and we could start inside…"

wires, starting from the roof and working downwards. I cut and fitted all of the noggins, setting them at the right heights for the switches and electrical outlets. I'm a bit of a perfectionist, so I worked out exactly where I wanted things, measuring exactly so that, for example, in the kitchen I would be able to get a tile and a half under the sockets. It took a bit of doing, especially as we hadn't yet bought the kitchen and the floor finishes weren't in but, by and large, I got it right."

Phil and Caroline had taken out an Accelerator mortgage, which allowed them to stay in their old house for the majority of the build. Once the wiring was complete and tested out they were able to run a cable through to the new house, meaning that Phil could work there in the evenings.

▲ **The cosy lounge has a glorious woodburning stove, situated in an imposing brick fireplace.**

▶

◀ **Despite the need for space efficiency in a low cost build, Phil and Caroline have managed to incorporate a spacious landing.**

With work progressing rapidly, the couple decided that they could put the old house on the market. It sold a lot quicker than they had calculated and, as they didn't want to lose the sale, they had to de-camp to a small touring caravan in their garden for the last few weeks of the build.

"We fitted the kitchen ourselves, with a little help from the builder, and the two of us got stuck into the decoration," says Phil. "Everything was going really smoothly. Then I had a rotten accident. We have used plastic plumbing and it was all tested out and working perfectly before the builders went on holiday. I was fixing up the speaker cables and I drilled straight through a pipe, causing a major leak that ruined the kitchen ceiling! I got some stick over it from Caroline but in the end we just had to buckle to and put it right.

"Everything was going really smoothly. Then I had a rotten accident…"

"It caused a bit of a delay, as did the service connections. I had put in all of the pipework for the gas points and, in view of my job, I had taken on full responsibility, but that didn't mean that it wasn't a hassle at times. The services didn't come from the old house. They came all the way down the new entrance. When Transco came, the scaffolding was still up so I had to hand dig the last seven metres through to the meter boxes myself.

"All in all it's been a wonderful experience. We were lucky with the people we chose and the companies we worked with. I'm proud of my schedules and programmes. In the end they were just about spot on and I feel that the success of this project has been the forward planning that we did. That and the wonderful chance that we were given by that casual conversation with our neighbour." ■

Useful Contacts

Architect – Elliott & Edwards Project Management:	01229 580088
Timber Frame – Guardian Homes Ltd.:	01772 614243
Builders – Coward & Kerr Builders:	01229 828004
Plumber – Mark Maguire:	01229 431225
Roofer – Kendall Bros.:	01229 430701
Finance – Accelerator from Buildstore:	0870 870 9991

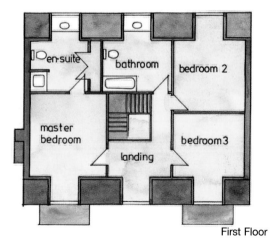

First Floor

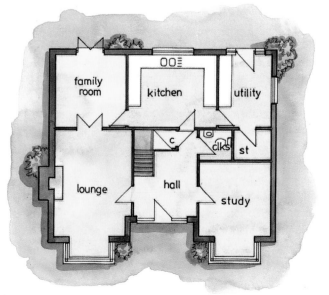

Ground Floor

Fact File *costs as of May 2002*

NAMES: Phil and Caroline Pearson	**CONSTRUCTION:** Timber frame
PROFESSIONS: Maintenance Strategy Engineer/Housewife	**WARRANTY:** Architect's Certificate
AREA: Cumbria	**FINANCE:** Accelerator Mortgage
HOUSE TYPE: Detached 3 bed chalet	**BUILD TIME:** Feb – Oct 2000
HOUSE SIZE: 176m²	**LAND COST:** £5,000
BUILD ROUTE: Subcontractors	**BUILD COST:** £85,000
	TOTAL COST: £90,000
	HOUSE VALUE: £140,000
	COST/m²: £482

36% COST SAVING

DIY Lawyers

Taking on the task of conveyancing sounds daunting but self-builders Graham Sharp and Judith Watson found that it was much easier than they expected and saved themselves £1,000 into the bargain.

▲ "It's really a matter of common sense," says Graham, who with his partner Judith took on the legal work on their plot purchase, saving themselves time and money. "You can get the forms from legal stationers."

Graham Sharp and Judith Watson have spent nearly five years self-building their £250,000 eco friendly house overlooking the English Channel. They and their daughter, Katy, are now looking forward to finally moving in, even though it's not quite finished.

They bought the land for £35,000 around six years ago after selling their London house and moving into a two bedroom terrace near the site. Since then they've spent about £70,000 on building the new house, doing everything either themselves or with the help of others. What we wanted to talk to them about was the 'white collar' trade of conveyancing that Judith did herself.

What made you decide to do this?

I'd worked as a legal secretary in a temporary job while I was studying, so knew how easy it was. I did the conveyancing on the sale of the London house as well as the purchase of our present house and this land. I used a book called *The Conveyancing Fraud* by Michael Joseph as a guide. It's a bit idiosyncratic and full of his opinions but the main things you need to know are in there.

What are the first things you need to do or know?

You need to know that this is the property you want to buy. Are the boundaries as described? We went and spoke to the neighbours on both sides and at the bottom to ask if there were any problems or disputes that they knew of. We went to see the local authority to check the planning and also things like smoke control regulations and sewage requirements. We investigated the soil conditions and spoke to the Building Control department about them. We went to see the Engineer's department to find out about drains and investigated services, in particular Southern Water. On the planning, we weren't just interested in this site but in all applications or proposals in the neighbourhood.

Surely these are things that everybody should do?

They are but so often when people use professionals they leave it up to them and they're not the ones who should be making the decisions. Anyway, it's the purchaser who has to prepare the draft contract and that's the next real stage.

You get the forms from legal stationers. They're a standard form of contract including a standard draft of preliminary enquiries and local search forms to be filled in. It's a con, you know — all the solicitor really has to do is look up the name and address of the local authority. If you want to ask any additional questions, there's room on the form and then they're sent off to the vendors or their solicitors. The replies, when they come back, are anodyne anyway. If they don't know they say so and even if they do, they might reply 'not known'. Covenants and easements need checking out but, in reality, many of them are either lapsed or unenforcable. It's really a matter of common sense. In the end, it's down to you to check things out. Then, when and only when you're sure, you can exchange contracts.

You do have a problem over the deposit because a solicitor won't trust you as he would another solicitor. I tried to set up a joint account but he wouldn't have that, so in the end we just had to send him the cheque and agree, once it was cashed, that the exchange had taken place.

At this stage, having exchanged contracts, are you committed?

Yes, but you need to confirm that they can, in fact, sell you the land. The fact that the Land Registry is now open means that you can find all of this out with relative ease. The registration lists the legal owners and gives details of any charges, covenants and easements affecting the land. The Land Registry are very helpful — if there are any issues that you are unsure of, you only have to ask.

Completion comes along and for that you need a banker's draft or building society cheque. If you needed a mortgage, your building society would want to have their own solicitor for the Deed of Mortgage. If you use a solicitor, they often act in both roles but not necessarily. All a solicitor would do is copy the searches, Land Registry details and answers to enquiries to them, so it's not that difficult.

Is that it then?

No, within three months you have to register the title and pay any Stamp Duty that's payable. The forms for registering the title are available from the Land Registry and you send those with the transfer and mortgage deeds.

And the savings?

Typically, between £600 and £1,000 per transaction! ∎

"You can get the forms from legal stationers…all the solicitor has to do is look up the address of the local authority…"

Words: **Debbie Jeffery**   Photography: **Jeremy Phillips**

Second Time Self-build

John and Christine Hambleton have used the experience gained on their first project to create an elegant new timber frame home.

Building a bespoke timber frame home

"This isn't our first foray into self-build," says John Hambleton. "About 27 years ago we bought a small piece of land where we built a brick and block bungalow." John had worked in the construction industry for ICI and managed the project himself – living in the property with Christine and their three children for the next 25 years. When the orchard belonging to a neighbouring farmhouse came onto the market the Hambletons decided to purchase the third of an acre to use as additional garden for their grandchildren to enjoy. Many games of cricket were played in the grounds, and only recently did the couple consider building themselves a smaller home on the land.

They preferred the idea of a well insulated timber framed house, and were inspired by Potton's site of show houses in St Neots. "We liked the Caxton from their Tudor style Heritage range," says Christine, "and felt that it would suit the plot extremely well." Situated about 12 miles from Chester, Sutton Weaver is a small hamlet with only a few hundred inhabitants. "The neighbouring farmhouse was built in 1778, and our new house stands on the site of a thatched labourer's cottage, which was demolished in the 1960s," Christine recalls. "We're not modernists, and found the sloping bedroom ceilings and exposed post and beam interiors of the Caxton appealing and full of character. It seemed perfect for this setting."

▲ The Hambletons' new house has been constructed in the garden of their bungalow — which they also built themselves.

▶

"I could certainly have done with the sort of backup [that Potton gave us] first time around!"

Concealed ▲ electric floor and ceiling heating ensure that the house remains at a constant, comfortable temperature.

John and Christine had initially planned to build themselves a smaller home, but their new house is actually larger than the previous bungalow — although it has been designed to better suit their needs. The standard Caxton has been modified to include a sunroom, vaulted ceilings in the master bedroom and an extra computer room above the garage in addition to the four bedrooms in the main house. With the land fronting onto a main road the Hambletons proposed to fill their site across the front by incorporating an integral garage, and lengthening the house to abut the boundaries on either side. "We feel very secure knowing that no-one can wander round to the rear of the house without us knowing," says Christine.

"When we built the bungalow we didn't have the money to employ an architect and simply adapted the set of plans which came with the site," says John. "I now realise that these drawings weren't detailed enough, and would advise anyone embarking on a self-build to have a thorough understanding of exactly how the house will be constructed.

The large ▶ inglenook fireplace houses a solid fuel stove and features herringbone pattern brickwork.

"We certainly had no such worries with Potton, as the detailed drawings and specifications are all part of the package, and we were allocated a project manager who we could turn to for advice — which gives you a great deal of confidence. I could certainly have done with that sort of back-up the first time around!"

John had already tested the water by applying for planning permission for a dwelling on the plot which, ▶

"I'm 68, but I've not given up — there may still be another self-build in me yet!"

The creamy ▲ yellow Shaker style kitchen units from John Lewis of Hungerford include free-standing dressers next to the Aga.

although technically Green Belt, backing onto open fields and close to listed buildings, was classed as an infill site. "We didn't really like the design, and neither did the planners," he says, "but there were precedents nearby and they could find no grounds on which to turn it down. I think they were rather relieved when they saw what we actually wanted to build!" The previous owner of the land had placed a covenant on the garden preventing further development which the Hambletons needed to purchase prior to building — costing a total of £80,000.

Once again, John decided that he would manage the project, tackling some of the hands-on work himself including laying the drains, labouring for the bricklayers, fitting the central vacuum system and decorating. When the split level bungalow was built he had set out the site using string and boards, and saw no reason to change his method for the Potton house. "It probably took far longer than using a theodolite, but the builders were impressed at just how accurate it all was," says John. "In some ways we were very naïve," he laughs. "Designing a split level property created a few problems, but we managed to over-come them and I was able to put my knowledge to good use this time."

The Potton frame took a matter of days to erect and was clad using new York Handmade bricks and clay roof tiles, reclaimed from an old sanitorium. Local subcontractors were employed to complete the project, with John on site every day labouring alongside them. With more money ▶

The kitchen ▶ floor tiles are from York Handmade Brick.

▲ One of the main appeals of the Potton design for John and Christine was the post and beam features.

available at this time in their lives the Hambletons opted for a far higher specification on their Potton home — including a whole house ventilation system with heat recovery and a built-in vacuum.

One important aspect of the Potton house is the zoned electric underfloor and ceiling heating from ESWA. "I think that, considering the Romans were pumping hot water around their buildings, the method is probably a

little archaic by now," laughs John, who saw the ceiling heating demonstrated in the Caxton showhome. "I would be concerned about fitting a wet underfloor heating system in case of leaks, but the electric heating needs absolutely no maintenance and is efficient and very cost effective to run."

Ceiling heating using foils — flexible heating elements of approximately 0.2mm thick — provides full heating in the first floor rooms, with heating cables embedded into the solid ground floors offering ESWA's 'Up and Under' — a combination of the two systems which may be run on special storage heating electricity tariffs. "Our terracotta tiles and oak flooring work extremely well with the underfloor heating," says Christine. "We certainly wouldn't go back to the combi boiler and radiators we fitted in our old bungalow."

After all their hard work the retired couple should be relaxing in their new sunroom and enjoying the fruits of their labour. When asked whether they would ever consider building again, however, John looks slightly sheepish and admits to recently viewing a plot in a nearby village.

"We do love it here," he says, "but if we found another piece of land we would consider building a slightly smaller Potton house and then perhaps letting our daughter and her husband move in here. I'm 68, but I've not given up — there may still be another self-build in me yet!" ∎

Fact File costs as of Oct 2002

NAMES: John & Christine Hambleton

PROFESSIONS: Retired

AREA: Cheshire

HOUSE TYPE: Four bedroom house

HOUSE SIZE: 198m^2

BUILD ROUTE: Self-managed/timber frame kit

CONSTRUCTION: Potton timber frame, blockwork outer leaf

WARRANTY: Zurich Custombuild

FINANCE: Private

BUILD TIME: 18 months

LAND COST: £80,000	
BUILD COST: £126,000	**41% COST SAVING**
TOTAL COST: £206,000	
HOUSE VALUE: £350,000	
COST/m^2: £636	

Cost Breakdown:

Planning and building regs	£4,500
Insurance	£900
Services	£1,300
Substructure/foundations	£3,500
Site clearance	£3,600
Drains	£1,500
Potton kit	£37,000
Scaffolding	£1,300
Bricks and labour	£14,000
Roofing materials/labour	£8,000
Lintels	£300
Dry Lining/insulation	£6,000
Rendering	£1,500
Electric heating inc water	£2,000
Heat recovery + ventilation	£1,300
Kitchen and aga	£14,500
Light fittings	£1,500
Garage doors	£1,200
Painting + decorating	£2,000
Oak floors inc. laying	£3,500
Wood panelling	£600
Paving and labour	£3,000
Miscellaneous	£13,000
TOTAL	**£126,000**

USEFUL CONTACTS: **Timber frame kit** - Potton Ltd: 01480 401401; **Rainwater goods** - Travis Perkins: 0161 7368751; **Underfloor and ceiling heating** - ESWA Ltd: 020 7582 4300; **Ultra-Vac central vacuum system** - Renvac Ltd: 01469 574300; **Akor heat recovery system** - Hampton Environmental Systems Ltd.: 01635 569933; **AGA**-Rayburn: 08457 125207; **Warranty** Zurich Custombuild : 01252 522000; **Bricks and floor tiles** - York Handmade Brick Co: 01347 838881; **Artisan kitchen** - John Lewis of Hungerford: 0700 2784726; **Sanitaryware** - Homebase: 0870 900 8098; **Oak flooring** - Shrewsbury Timber: 01630 685777; **Roofer** - Reportsite: 01928 787804; **Joiner/builder** - Ardent Joinery Ltd: 01925 262524; **Mortar** - Tilcon: 01964 542453

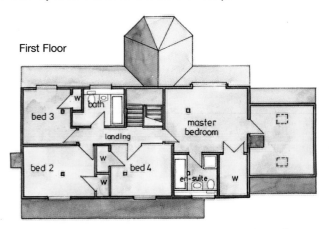

First Floor

FLOORPLAN: The Hambletons modified Potton's four bedroom Caxton design to incorporate a ground floor sunroom and an integral garage with a room above. Their dining room and fourth bedroom have been enlarged so that the house runs across the full width of the site.

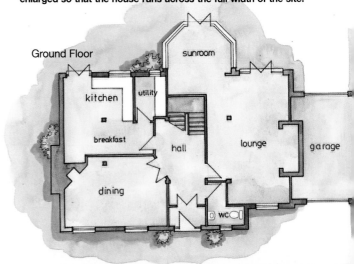

Ground Floor

DIY Roofing

Mark and Janis Button are building close to the White Cliffs of Dover and doing a lot of the work themselves. H&R spoke to them about having a go at the roof tiling which they hope will save them £2,500.

Janis and Mark Button are building a four bedroom, chalet style home near the Kent coast. As Mark's busy holding down a full time job whilst trying to manage the build, they've elected to use a package deal company, Design & Materials Ltd, for the supply of the materials.

The land, which they found through a local estate agent, cost them £25,000. Although they have a long way to go yet, Mark estimates that the total cost of their project will come in at around £80,000. If you set that against a finished value of £120,000, then they're certainly due to be rewarded financially for all the hard work, long nights and lost weekends.

Amongst the tasks that Mark is doing on a DIY self-build basis, to help keep costs down, is laying all of the rooftiles himself. H&R asked him how it went and if he had any tips or advice for others hoping to do the same.

Did you have any previous experience of roof tiling?

No and, to cap it all, I'm not very good with heights, but I've just had to get used to it. I realised that I'd need some help and, although I've done the bulk of the work myself, I did get a tiler friend to give me some tips. Unfortunately that didn't save me a lot of wasted time when, instead of cutting a gauge for the spacing of the battening, I used a tape and a level, only to find that my level was out. I had to go back down to the first row and start again and it meant I got a few extra, unwanted holes in the felt.

We're using a concrete interlocking tile, the Redland Mini Stonewold and, with the exposure rating we have, it meant that every tile has to be nailed twice and clipped, which is quite time consuming.

My friend taught me how to gauge the tiles across the roof so that we ended up, on a straight run, with a half tile at the verge. At first I thought that this would mean a lot more cutting with the angle grinder but then he showed me a technique which involves laying one tile over another and then cracking hard down on the centre line with the edge of another tile. If you do that, they split in half quite cleanly.

Was it physically hard work bumping out and did you load out the roof before you started?

It is hard work and, if you're on your own, it slows down the job considerably. What we have to contend with here is the wind. We're only a short distance from the White Cliffs and I felt that it wouldn't be a good idea to load the whole roof. Anyway, I'm slower than a professional tiler so I found it easier to load out about 50 tiles onto the scaffold and take from there. With a roof like this, with dormers and Velux windows creating an interruption every few metres, I had to keep stopping and starting and coming back down to the scaffold in any event. What does hurt are the muscles in your calf which you're stretching all the time and I did find that I wore out two pairs of trainers on their sides quite quickly.

Will you be doing your own leadwork around the dormers?

No. I've decided against that and the plumber will be cutting and laying it for me. We're using fibreglass valleys to the dormers and I've decided to shiplap the dormer cheeks instead of tiling them. The only real problem I've had with the dormers is the barge board where, until my friend pointed it out to me, I hadn't cut it short enough at the angle where it meets the roof to allow for the fact that two thicknesses of tile need to run under it.

I have also had a bit of a problem with the side flashing for the Velux windows and I haven't managed to fully resolve it yet, despite talking several times to their technical depart-

"I'm not very good with heights but I've just had to get used to it...I did get a tiler friend to give me some tips!"

ment. I've checked that I've got the windows set into the roof at the right level but the side flashing with its compressible strip still tends to kick up the tile. We're using Redland's dry ridge system which should save me days and which I specified because of the wind factor. I've seen what happens to a bedded ridge in this area.

What tips would you give other self-builders thinking of tiling?

A straight up and over roof is easy but, if you've got dormers, then have a chat with a professional first. Everyone said it would be easy but when you hit a dormer every four rows I can assure you it's not. You need a good ladder and a good scaffold and I'd recommend that you get some proper kneepads. If you're cutting tiles with an angle grinder make sure that you're wearing gloves, goggles and a mask — those things can be really dangerous. Also, get a diamond blade. It'll be about £30 more but that's nothing compared to the time I have saved! ■

Retired housebuilder Brian Barnett's final project
was a new home for himself and wife Loretta,
created using an oak frame reclaimed from an
18th Century barn.

Words:
Michael Holmes

Photography:
Nigel Rigden

Old timber barns tend to come with lots of potential and plenty of character. Unfortunately – as new owners very quickly find out – they also tend to come with lots of design constraints. The siting and orientation are a fait accompli; the planners usually want to see as few alterations to the original structure as possible, limiting the number of new window and door openings; then there is the cost of working with an old structure in situ – far greater than building from scratch thanks to underpinning, damp proofing, timber treatment, retro fitting insulation and so on.

Given its sensitive green belt location near Kingswood, Surrey, and close proximity to a Grade II listed farmhouse, you would expect Brian and Loretta Barnett to have experienced all manner of problems when they turned their mid 18th Century oak barn into a beautiful three bedroom home – but then theirs is no ordinary barn conversion. Although the frame is well over a century old, it only arrived in its current location three years ago and is technically, therefore, a new house and as such free of the usual planning constraints.

Brian and Loretta purchased the barn from Peter Barker of Antique Buildings Ltd, a firm which specialises in reclaimed oak and elm frames salvaged from all over the British Isles. At his yard in Dunsfold, Surrey, Peter has a selection of frames of all shapes and sizes, ranging from old cowsheds, to hovels and barns. The Barnetts' frame, which cost them £16,000, originally housed cattle on a ▶

Final Frame

A new home built from an old barn

The chimney ▶
and brick inglenook
were all built using
local bricks from
Chelwood Brick.

The windows ▶
were all made
from new oak.
Great care was
taken to line up
the frames with
timbers of the
barn.

"It made sense to turn the accommodation upside down, with the first floor given over to one large living area."

farm near Lingfield, around twelve miles from Kingswood. "When we first set eyes on it, it was nothing more than a pile of timber accompanied by a few photographs and some measurements," recalls Brian.

"The outline planning permission on our site had only been granted on appeal, as a replacement for an existing rundown cottage. Given the Green Belt location, one of the planning conditions was that the new dwelling be no more than ten percent larger in volume than the original. The frame we bought, measuring 12m x 6m plus an outshot, was more or less a perfect match for what we were allowed."

With the exception of the sole plates, which had been in contact with the ground, the frame was in good ▶

156

The ground floor is covered in Chinese slate and the first floor in ceramic quarry tiles. Both are warmed by a Nu-Heat underfloor heating system.

The simple, rustic ▲ style painted kitchen units were made by local carpenter David How for half the cost of a designer brand name kitchen. The black, all electric range style cooker is a Britannia.

Fact File costs as of July 2001

NAME: Brian and Loretta Barnett

PROFESSION: Retired

AREA: Kingswood, Surrey

HOUSE TYPE: Three bed detached using reclaimed oak barn frame

HOUSE SIZE: 140m²

BUILD ROUTE: Local Subcontractors

CONSTRUCTION: Oak frame, brick, flints and timber cladding

WARRANTY: NHBC

SAP RATING: Unknown

FINANCE: Private

BUILD TIME: May '98–Sept '99

LAND COST: £150,000

BUILD COST: £150,080

TOTAL COST: £300,080

HOUSE VALUE: £950,000

COST/M²: £1,072

68% COST SAVING

Useful Contacts

Architect — Norman Franklin & Associates: 0208 8688 1410

Reclaimed Oak Frame — Antique Buildings Ltd: 01483 200477

Frame erection and restoration — Gary Wood: 01737 842533

Bricks — Chelwood: 0161 485 8211

Rooftiles — Tudor Roof Tile Co Ltd: 01797 320202

Underfloor Heating — Nu-Heat Ltd: 01395 578482

Conservation Rooflights — The Velux Co: 01592 772211

Oak Doors — British Gates & Timber: 01580 291555

Woodburning Stove – Dorking Stove Co: 01306 883201

Kitchen – David How: 01306 611092

Range Cooker – Britannia: 01253 471111

condition. These were replaced in their entirety using 8" x 6" sections of green oak. "We also had to replace the lean to section of the barn to create the third bedroom and lean to overhang for the log store," explains Brian. "I would say that you have to allow a figure of around twenty percent on top of the price of the frame for replacement oak. None the less, this route has lots of advantages compared to converting an existing barn. It would have been more expensive to have worked in situ.

"With a project like this, it is essential to find someone who knows about barn construction," Brian advises. "We phoned several firms and were lucky enough to find an experienced master carpenter, Gary Wood, who took great pains to get things right and really was first class."

The Barnetts' frame was first rebuilt in sections laid flat out on the ground to ensure that all of the parts were complete and the joints in working order. Any missing or damaged timbers were repaired or replaced using either reclaimed oak or new green oak which Gary hand adzed to give an aged effect. The whole structure was then treated, before being dismantled and erected once more, stick by stick, with each joint held together using freshly cut oak pegs. Three years on, it is very difficult to distinguish repair from original, or old from new. ▶

The structure is
insulated entirely
outside the frame
rather than in between
the timbers leaving
the oak frame
exposed as a feature
on the inside.

"Given the restricted volume we had to work with, it would have been impossible to create double height spaces and still make the most of the timber roof structure. It therefore made sense to turn the accommodation upside down, with the first floor given over to one large open plan living area, making the most of the barn roof and the views over the surrounding countryside," explains Brian. "Once we had made this decision, the rest of the house designed itself around the shape of the frame."

In spite of his prior experience, Brian decided to bring on board an architect to fine tune the design and handle the planning process. "You can get too close to these things," he says, "plus my architect, Norman Franklin, is well known to the local planners who trust his work. His reputation inevitably helped in the negotiations. I also brought on board a structural engineer to prove that the frame was up to the job."

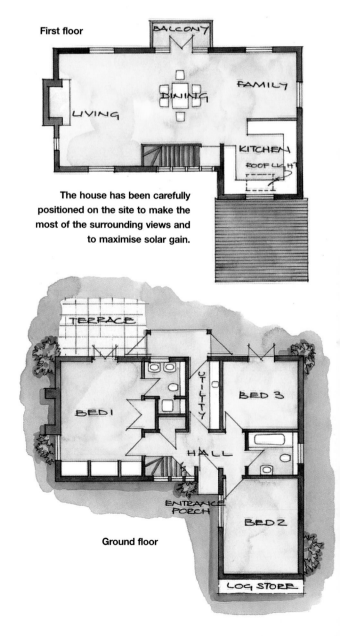

First floor

The house has been carefully positioned on the site to make the most of the surrounding views and to maximise solar gain.

Ground floor

"Norman subtly reminded [the planners] that this was, after all, a new house and not a barn conversion."

▲ The irregular size and shape of the clay tiles – a combination of three different colours from Tudor Tile Co – lend the building considerable character, helping it to look established in its setting. The traditional knapped flint walls, chimney and plinth were built by Roger Bastone, now retired.

In order to create the ceiling heights necessary for two storeys, the frame was erected on top of a 1200mm blockwork plinth which is clad in knapped flint panels with brick surrounds from the local Chelwood brickworks. The exterior of the oak frame is clad in large section feather edged boarding, stained black.

"One feature which the planners did object to was the chimney — which they claimed was not in keeping with a barn," says Brian. "However, Norman managed to persuade them that the design would be sympathetic to the character of the building and subtly reminded them that this was, after all, a new house and not a barn conversion."

"The original budget for the build was £100,000, but we ended up spending £150,000," says Brian. "Much of the extra cost went on the quality of the materials, such as the Tudor Handmade clay tiles, flint panels and so on, but they are worth every penny.

"My advice for anyone trying to undertake a project like this is not to try and do it on a shoestring," he advises. "The building dictates to you and you can't cut corners – it would stand out like a sore thumb if, for instance, you put in a standard softwood staircase instead of oak. The only downside to a house like this is that there is nowhere to hang pictures in amongst all of the beams, but then they are a feature in their own right!" ■

SUBSCRIBE NOW - SAVE 30%

1 year for £35.70 — SAVE 15% (£6.30)

● *Equivalent to just £2.98 per issue (£3.50 per issue in the shops)*

2 years for £58.80 — SAVE 30% (£25.20)

● *Equivalent to just £2.45 per issue (£3.50 per issue in the shops)*

Homebuilding & Renovating magazine is an invaluable read for anyone who is considering, just starting or in the middle of extending, renovating, converting or building their own home.

Established as a trusted authority on all aspects of building and renovating, Homebuilding & Renovating successfully blends a 'how to' practical approach with an aspirational 'can do' outlook.

SUBSCRIBERS BENEFITS

- ■ **FREE** access to the Exclusive Magazine Subscribers Area at www.homebuilding.co.uk
- ■ Special discounts on other H&R products (see below)
- ■ **FREE** pair of tickets to all H&R Shows (worth up to £104)

● All subscribers will have **FREE** access to the whole of the new **www.homebuilding.co.uk** site. The site includes hundreds of readers' homes, houseplans, product information, advice on finance and planning plus the full Beginner's Guide and Complete Self-builder series.

ORDER YOUR SUBSCRIPTION OR BOOKS NOW:

- ■ online at **www.homebuilding.co.uk/shop** (Save an extra £1 when you subscribe online)
- ■ or call our order hotline **01527 834435**

ALL THE HELP YOU NEED FOR YOUR BUILD

Book of Contemporary Homes

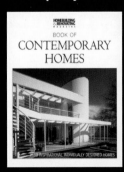

19 unique contemporary style homes in full colour. An invaluable source of inspiration for anyone planning to build. Remarkable projects built from £60,000 to £1 million plus.

ONLY £14.95 plus £2.50 p&p
SUBSCRIBER PRICE £12.99 inc p&p

The Homebuilder's Handbook

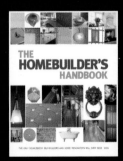

Featuring 1000's of contact details, this is the ultimate sourcebook for anyone planning to renovate, convert or build their own home. Comprehensive coverage from bricks to bathrooms.

ONLY £19.99 (RRP £24.99 + £5 p&p)
SUBSCRIBER PRICE ONLY £15 inc p&p

How to Renovate a House in France

An essential guide to help you turn an old rural property in France into a beautiful home. It covers the whole process, from assessing and buying a property, through all the jobs required to get it into shape.

ONLY £25 inc p&p worth £5

Find Your Perfect Plot of Land
www.plotfinder.net
ONLINE LAND AND RENOVATION DATABASE

LAND FOR SALE - **whether you are looking for a building plot, a property that needs renovating or a place to convert into a home, www.plotfinder.net can make your search easier and save you time.**

- **www.plotfinder.net** is a database which holds details of **over 5,500** building plots and properties for renovation currently for sale in the UK.

- All the time and effort required to find a plot is done for you, which means you will have more time to enjoy planning and designing your dream home.

Subscribe to www.plotfinder.net
One year subscription ONLY £40!

- FREE email alert when new plots are added to your chosen counties.
- Unlimited access to the www.plotfinder.net database for any five counties.
- Save favourite plots into separate folder.
- Mark viewed plots as read.
- The website gives you instant access to plot details (updated hourly).

NEW - **www.sitefinderireland.com** is a new sister site to plotfinder.net
LOG ON NOW to find your ideal building site or renovation project in Ireland

*Price as at August 2004, we withold the right to change this price at any time.